Iain Wightwick is a barrister at Unity Street Chambers in Bristol. He is a specialist property lawyer, with particular interest in landlord and tenant issues and in general work, especially social housing with a focus on neighbour nuisance and related anti-social behaviour matters ('neighbours from hell'), housing disrepair, homelessness, general social and private sector housing law.

This is his second book. He wrote *"A Practical Guide to Antisocial Behaviour Injunctions"* in 2019.

He has thirty years' experience of acting for social landlords and tenants and a reputation for creative, cost-controlling approaches to litigation and to alternative dispute resolution.

He has been instructed to advise and appear in many disrepair claims, mostly for landlords but sometimes for tenants. He has a unique approach to the issues amongst his colleagues, which centres around the need to enable social landlords to provide quality accommodation rather than pay lawyers' fees.

Shortly after the first Housing Disrepair Protocol was published, he concluded that tenants should be directed to alternative dispute resolution rather than instructing solicitors to pursue the steps in the Housing Conditions Protocol. That approach has saved his clients very substantial sums in legal fees, which he hopes has benefited the tenants of those landlords.

He is always available, whether for a chat about a legal issue or about a mountain bike ride/open water swim/ski.

A Practical Guide to Responding to Housing Disrepair and Unfitness Claims

A Practical Guide to Responding to Housing Disrepair and Unfitness Claims

Policies, Processes and Practice in Responding to Disrepair and Unfitness Claims

Iain Wightwick, BSc Hons, Dip. Law
Barrister, Unity Street Chambers, Bristol

Law Brief Publishing

Published 2021 by Law Brief Publishing, an imprint of Law Brief Publishing Ltd
30 The Parks
Minehead
Somerset
TA24 8BT

www.lawbriefpublishing.com

Paperback: 978-1-914608-16-2

This book is dedicated to:

*All those who have put up with me during
the writing of this book, but particularly
my wife and my children who have
supported my efforts throughout the slog.*

PREFACE

Disrepair (or more properly "housing conditions") claims are on the rise. This book should be helpful to those receiving and responding to them.

Such claims increased by 44% between 2012 and 2017 in England and Wales and they have continued to proliferate. In those five years Southwark LBC paid out about £10,000,000 in damages and costs. Sheffield City Council has disclosed that it has spent more than £1 million fighting disrepair claims within the last 2 ½ years. There has been a 322% increase in cases, which they blame on claims management companies using "aggressive marketing tactics" to attract tenants who are unhappy about the state of their homes during the pandemic. That has been greatly exacerbated by the inability on the part of all landlords to do repairs other than urgent works.

Housing conditions claims are not just wasteful in terms of officer time and finances. They can be very stressful for those involved, particularly where landlords face large numbers of claims and their staff are already busy planning and carrying out repairs, maintenance and improvements. I anticipate that all landlords would prefer to direct their resources to repairs rather than legal fees.

The book is more about the strategies needed to deal with disrepair litigation rather than the substantive law.

If you are a tenant's representative, I hope that the book will help you to weed out good claims from the many which are at present gratuitously and unnecessarily issued.

Fortunately, the Court of Appeal has just handed down a very helpful decision on an application for permission to appeal. In Hockett v Bristol City Council (2021) unreported, Ref: B2/2021/1025, Lord Justice Bean agreed with the approach which I conceived a number of years ago, and which has been approved of by many judges in the County Court.

I hope that the application of that philosophy to disrepair claims will dramatically reduce the legal bills currently being paid by social landlords. Many of the complaints which tenants are making about housing conditions should never have involved lawyers. You'll need to buy the book to find out more about it though!

The book also addresses how to respond to a disrepair claim in the event that ADR is not appropriate or fails to appease the tenant.

The law described in this book is believed to be correct and up-to-date at 1st September 2021.

Iain Wightwick
September 2021

STOP PRESS:

After the publishers had typeset the book, the Ministry of Justice confirmed that it is going to implement fixed costs in the fast track and in most money claims up to the value of £25,000, on a date to be fixed.

Fast track claims will fall into four bands of complexity, Bands 1-4 from the least simplest case to the most technical and complicated. Fixed sums will be awarded depending on the stage which the proceedings have reached: pre-issue, post-issue, post-allocation, pre-listing or post-listing, pre-trial. There will be additional trial advocacy fees payable. Tracked possession claims and housing conditions/disrepair are likely to be categorised as Band 3, or Band 4 if more complicated.

This means that, roughly speaking, in cases where damages are less than £10,000, the recoverability of pre-issue costs will be substantially reduced, from the figures we see at present of £5,000-£10,000 to between about £1,000 and £2,250 plus 12.5-17.5% of damages. Total fees going to trial, excluding advocacy will be limited to about another

£11,000-£15,000 plus 20-40% of damages. Trial fees will be between £500 and £2,500 for the advocate. Currently those costs are usually claimed at £20,000-£35,000. The total recoverable costs will therefore fall for whoever wins.

While this is welcome news, it does not deal with the major problem of resource allocation caused by housing disrepair claims, because they will all still have to be investigated, and if they are not resolved through the landlord's internal complaints process, will necessitate the instruction of lawyers, either to negotiate a settlement or to defend them. In my experience, settling unmeritorious claims as a commercial decision usually results in the receipt of numerous additional claims, so even if the individual sum of costs recoverable falls.

ACKNOWLEDGEMENTS

This book has been another grind, written during weekends, so once again my family has suffered from my somewhat short-tempered attention to the writing. I am very grateful for their unstinting support and help, despite my occasional mutterings about lost time off.

CONTENTS

TABLE OF CASES

TABLE OF LEGISLATION

INTRODUCTION

Of the many claims being pursued, some are entirely justified. This book is not designed to help bad landlords 'get off'. There is a body of lawyers working tirelessly on behalf of disadvantaged tenants who are forced by unscrupulous landlords to live in appalling conditions. Those lawyers provide an essential service to our society, and I support them fully. Some tenants may endure appalling conditions, unaware of their remedies or too scared to use them until helped by lawyers. The legislation which protects them, in combination with their tenancy conditions, can be used to great effect to improve their lives.

There are others who also strive on behalf of tenants, but who have often obtained their clients through cold-calling, advertising on Facebook, approaching people on the streets and by other methods used by claims management companies to generate leads. Although cold-calling has been outlawed, as I write this book there are still cases in the pipeline in which the tenants were approached by people knocking on their doors as they sat at home. I have come across cases in which the tenant invited them in and showed them round, unaware that they were not surveyors sent by their landlord.

The claims management companies who generate these cases tend to focus on the social housing sector, for reasons to be discussed later. As a result, this book is more likely to be of use to social landlords, although I hope it will be useful to the private sector as well.

Turning to the history of these cases, a housing lawyer, I have represented both tenants and landlords over the past three decades and some, bringing and defending claims for what used to be called housing disrepair and is now better described as housing conditions.

In about 1992 I was first instructed to advise on defending them for one particular landlord. In those days there was no Pre-Action Protocol and often no warning that proceedings were on the way. Sometimes the first the landlord knew of a tenant's unhappiness with the repairs process was the receipt of the sealed court papers.

1

I realised fairly swiftly that what appeared to be allegations of serious and persistent breach of repairing duty were often no such thing. I was invariably asked how much in damages each tenant should be paid, so that the claims could be settled. But I began to suspect that landlords could not possibly be as uncaring and incompetent as they were painted in the pleadings.

My investigations with social landlord clients uncovered Repairs Teams who were surprised and probably annoyed that their legal teams were settling all claims received when they saw no reason to do so. They provided me with repairs histories, with evidence that they had repaired everything which the tenant had complained of, or sometimes almost everything. Often it transpired that, although the tenant's home might not be in perfect condition, there were myriad reasons for that and the fault did not lie at the landlord's door, or the damage might not be actionable.

It was a long and slow process learning how to defend those claims. Those involved with the repairs system provided witness statements and documents and I began to draft Defences. It was all a bit hit and miss. I did not even use a book on the subject, as we did not have a great library in those days. In 1996 I bought my copy of Stephen Knafler's excellent book, on the subject *"Remedies for Disrepair and Other Building Defects"*. Stephen Knafler sadly died in October 2020. He was only two months older than me, so I am 25 years behind him with this book.

The first edition of Dowding & Reynolds ("D & R") did not come out until 1994 and it was too expensive for me at that time. You will need to read the Preface to the Fifth Edition to understand that reference. D & R remains the practitioner's bible. This volume cannot begin to be any sort of replacement for that book and I trust that nobody is going to quote from this work in court.

And no practitioner should be without *"Housing Conditions, tenants' rights"* ("Housing Conditions") by HHJ Jan Luba QC, Catherine O'Donnell and Giles Peaker. D & R and Housing Conditions will provide you with the meat of the law – I only intend to provide bones and perhaps some gristle. There is no point in my trying to do anything more, because those two works are pretty much definitive on the substantive law. If you are going to Court on one of these claims, you will need access to the most recent edition of one or both of those books, as your opponent will almost certainly be quoting from them.

But, back in 1992, armed with ignorance and hope, we went to trial and we won, because not all landlords come from the school of Rachman. As things developed, so did the way of dealing with claims. It dawned on me that some cases were so hopeless that they should not even be allowed to go to trial. As the number of claims increased, so did the urgency of the problem, as claimant firms began to swamp landlords with claims. They were left unable to devote the resources necessary to fight them and legal bills escalated into the millions of pounds for many social landlords.

This book is a distillation of the ways in which you can test a claim which comes in, whether you are a lawyer asked to tackle it, a housing professional or a landlord trying to understand it. But better still, as a landlord I hope you can refine processes so that such claims never see the light of day, because no tenant will want to click on a Facebook advert which says: "Do you want your repairs done?"

The book approaches disrepair claims from the perspective of the Letter of Claim as that is the building block of disrepair litigation. This is misleading, as such letters should not be sent until a landlord has been told about outstanding repairs and has nevertheless failed to act. Further, Social housing tenants are also required to consider alternative dispute resolution, and the landlord's own complaints procedure is placed at the forefront of that suggestion.

More of that later, but for present purposes, please start to think of the Pre-Action Protocol for Housing Conditions as being more than just a formula that people must robotically follow before inevitably issuing proceedings. It provides the starting point for saying that lawyers should not be involved in a housing conditions claim unless it's unavoidable.

Like my first book on antisocial behaviour injunctions, there are bound to be many errors in this volume, both of spelling and grammar and, more important, in law and practice. Please do point them out to me, although preferably not in a humiliating fashion.

Best of luck in redirecting some at least of the money which currently goes into the pockets of lawyers (including me) into the repair of homes!

PART I

AVOIDING CLAIMS FOR DISREPAIR

Ideally, no tenant will ever be tempted to engage solicitors, because your estate management is so good that they cannot think of any reason why they would want to do so.

In that perfect world, your housing stock would be maintained so well that it does not have a chance to fall into disrepair, because it is inspected so frequently that maintenance is carried out proactively. Few property owners will ever even aspire to that level of investment, because it is not cost-effective. Good estate management is all about getting perfect balance between cost, which is ultimately borne by the tenants through their rent, and the standard of comfort they enjoy. At the other end of the scale, some landlords might only carry out work when the tenant asks them to attend, and then complete repairs which address the immediate problem without 'future proofing' the home.

There are varying degrees between the two extremes and landlords will make their repairs policies to fit their budget and rental philosophy. The standard to which properties must be kept is not fixed by law, because it depends on the type of accommodation. As a general rule, the higher the rent, the better the standard which needs to be set.

The size of the estate will, to an extent, dictate the systems employed by the landlord to administer it. The larger the number of properties, the more important it becomes to have a fool-proof and comprehensive policy.

This first section of the book is very short. I merely draw attention to the importance of comprehensive, up-to-date repairs policies and procedures, which you will use to prevent claims and to ensure that those made are unlikely to succeed.

A policy designed to respond to disrepair claims is also needed. This book is intended to give some idea of the nature of considerations pertinent to that policy.

CHAPTER ONE

ESTATE MANAGEMENT POLICIES

I do not anticipate that this book will be read by many landlords who do not have a management policy. Registered Providers must have policies and procedures in place. The claimant firms of solicitors tend to target social landlords, because they are seen as easier prey.

Why are they relevant to disrepair claims?

Although 'Estate Management' might include tenancy and environmental management, antisocial behaviour, successions, allocations and so on, this chapter is mainly concerned with maintenance and improvement policies, and the systems needed to support them.

Policies help employees to make decisions without management involvement and they ensure that there is a sufficient degree of consistency to avoid a haphazard approach to the control of the estate. When somebody complains that they have not been treated properly, the existence of a policy can benefit both parties.

The landlord can maintain an objective approach and will find it easier to be fair to all tenants. Tenants know the standards they can expect, and employees will be able to respond consistently to similar issues.

The degree of detail in these policies and procedures is a matter of judgement. In general, the larger the organisation, the more extensive the policies and procedures it needs. Staff members are more numerous and the number of properties in the estate will mean that there are more likely to be untoward or unusual events which need to be approached by all employees in the same way.

It is a question of maintaining a balance between an overly rigid or bureaucratic approach and giving staff the ability to be practical and use their judgement. In terms of the repairs policy, the fundamental guiding principle will be the standards which the landlord sets itself as a housing provider.

Policies will need to be reviewed and updated, both at regular intervals and following changes to key legislation, regulations or best practice guidelines. The aims of a landlord may change and the policy may become outdated, or on a performance review a housing provider may find that it is under-delivering and needs to tighten or improve policies.

In housing conditions law this is particularly pertinent. The coming into force of the Homes (Fitness for Human Habitation) Act 2018 has fundamentally changed the landscape in terms of repairs and improvements. Policies are almost certain to require change, to reflect the fact that merely repairing properties is no longer sufficient to avoid legal liability for substandard living conditions.

Updating policies

There is a real need for providers to take into account the changes imposed by the 2018 Act and other related legislation, and by the changes anticipated by the charter for social housing residents, the social housing White Paper, published on 17 November 2020.

The greatest danger to landlords is the setting of a quality standard which is too low to satisfy the law, or too high to be affordable. The Welfare Reform and Work Act 2016 forced social landlords to reduce their rents by 1% each year over the following four years. That led to numerous problems and many landlords suffered significant budgetary issues as a result.

In early 2019, the government agreed that social housing rents would be allowed to increase by the consumer price index measure of inflation +1% for the following five years from 2020. This should redress in part the imbalance caused by the previous policy, albeit only gradually. Almost every social landlord has raised its rent by the maximum permitted amount.

Some landlords will have changed their policies to reflect that reduction in rent, and they may now revert to the historic policies if changes were made to the standards set by the policies. The National Housing

Maintenance Forum is the best source of good practice for maintenance and asset management policies. It helps landlords both with policy and practical guidance to assist housing maintenance professionals.

Rather than discussing policies in detail, the purpose of this section of the book is to concentrate thought on the consequences of the wording of the landlord's repairs and maintenance policies.

Changes caused by the 2018 Act and other new statutes

Most important, such policies are no longer able to separate repairs and maintenance from improvements. The 2018 Act has necessitated a change to the fundamental approach to estate management. A property may be unfit for human habitation even though not in disrepair as defined by the 1985 Act. This means that works may be necessary even though they result in an improvement to the property rather than merely a repair to those parts of the property which a landlord has agreed to maintain.

The International Standard for Asset Management, ISO 55001, published in 2014, set a high bar, specifying requirements for the establishment, implementation, maintenance and improvement of an asset management system which can be used by any property owner. It does not mandate any financial, accounting or technical requirements for managing property, but gives guidance on the issues which need to be addressed in a policy.

Repairs and improvements policies

Such policies must be amended to take into account the effect of the 2018 Act. In general, social landlords encounter issues caused by the combination of housing stock with some peculiarities of construction with some tenants who struggle to make ends meet.

Complaints Policies

It is essential to operate an efficient and competent complaints policy. The current White Paper sets out goals for such policies in the future. The government intends them to play a much larger role in dispute resolution than is currently the case.

Your complaints policy, needs regular updating. If you do not have a policy, or the policy is not working, your first, urgent task should be to address that issue.

This book is not intended to go into detail on such policies, because they could form the subject of a separate book. For present purposes, I will assume that you either have a credible and efficient policy, or that, having read these lines, you are making all efforts to put one in place!

Such policies are important because of the part they should play in the relationship between social landlords and their tenants. Disrepair claims should not be fought out in County Courts all over the country as a matter of course. The legal system should be reserved exclusively for those cases where landlords have been asked, formally, to repair and have refused, and where the internal, formal Complaints Process has failed at all its stages to provide satisfactory resolution for the tenant.

But rather than starting with a detailed examination of the complaints process, we need to look at things from the point of view of a Letter of Claim. That is nearly always how a landlord is alerted to dissatisfaction on the part of their tenant. It is only in rare cases that a claimant tenant has repeatedly complained, or even used the Complaints Process and is still unhappy. Apart perhaps from suggesting that they go to the Ombudsman, in those cases there may be no alternative but to follow the steps in the Pre-Action Protocol and litigate if necessary.

Chapter Summary/Key Takeaways

- Policies set the tone of the organization

- They need to be updated regularly and in line with developments in the law, statute and society

- Setting the repairs standards in the policy will underpin most decision making in the asset management team

- Creating a customer-friendly Complaints Policy which is efficient and accurate in its determinations can and will save very substantial sums in legal costs and damages. All the money that is saved can be spent on the repairs and improvements which you and the tenants both want done.

In the remaining chapters you will learn how your asset management policy and your Complaints Policy help to determine how you answer the Letters of Claim which you will inevitably receive.

PART II

RESPONDING TO THE LETTER OF CLAIM

Even if your repairing policies are excellent, you are almost certain to get disrepair claims. The firms which bring claims against social landlords sometimes say on their websites that they will not pursue claims against private landlords. That is because, unlike many social landlords, they tend to fight claims aggressively. Therefore, however good you are at repairs, you need to know how to respond to claims, because claimant firms view social landlords as easy targets. Most of the remainder of this book will look at claims from a practical point of view, using the Letter of Claim ("LOC") as the springboard.

First we look at the origins and rationale of a LOC, which provide us with the chapter headings necessary to respond to a claim.

Of course, if the Protocol was used properly by claimant solicitors, unhappiness with repairs and housing conditions would not come to light with a Letter of Claim. Instead, first the tenant would give some form of formal notice to the landlord, whereupon the Complaints Policy can be put into operation. If that process fails, the tenant should go to the Ombudsman. Only if those measures are unsuccessful should a tenant need to engage lawyers.

In fact, paragraph 5.1 of the Protocol does say that "*In order to avoid unnecessary delay and to ensure that notice of the claim is given to the landlord of the earliest possible opportunity, particularly where repairs are urgent, it may be appropriate for the tenant to send a letter notifying the landlord of the claim before detailed Letter of Claim is sent*". Much of the time, such a letter would obviate the need for most of what subsequently is included in a LOC.

But, at the moment, things do not happen like that in England and Wales. Landlords receive Letters of Claim out of the blue and have to respond to them.

My approach to responding to such claims does not differ according to whether there is fault on the part of the landlord. If there is a breach of duty, it should be addressed by alternative dispute resolution, without the involvement of lawyers on either side, within the landlord's internal complaints process.

CHAPTER TWO

THE LETTER OF CLAIM

While the law of dilapidations is complex and sometimes bewildering and seemingly inconsistent even to lawyers, the Letter of Claim in a housing disrepair case provides a blueprint from which both sides can work toward the resolution of a claim.

Understanding and responding to an LOC is key to dealing with disrepair claims successfully.

The Rationale of the Housing Conditions/Disrepair Protocol

The Protocol came into force on 8 December 2003, so lawyers have been using – or misusing it for nearly 20 years. It is therefore surprising that the question of mandatory alternative dispute resolution has remained unresolved until 2021.

There are now two Protocols, one for England and one for Wales, where section 9A of the LTA 1985 has not been applied. So when I talk about the Protocol, in Wales practitioners will be referring to the version which contains no reference to unfitness, at least at the moment.

The idea of a Protocol was first raised during the Access to Justice enquiry, but social landlords and tenants' lawyers found it impossible to reach a consensus on its content. The Law Society eventually helped to achieve a measure of agreement.

The Protocol does not apply to counterclaims filed in possession proceedings. However, in those claims, tenants and landlords are still expected to act reasonably in exchanging information and trying to settle the case at an early stage (para 3.3). That can be important in terms of avoiding a trial.

The **Guidance to the Protocol** reminds tenants "to consider other options **before** using the protocol including the… Ombudsman".

Although the notes in the White Book say that if the claim is settled, the landlord should pay the tenant's costs and out-of-pocket expenses such as those incurred in small claims track cases, the claimant's Solicitors will normally try to insist on payment of costs on a Fast-Track basis, even if the amount of work done and compensation paid is minimal. This is the root of the current problem faced by social landlords from disrepair claims.

There is a case on the point – *Birmingham City Council v Lee* [2008] EWCA Civ 891, and it is essential reading for all those involved with such claims. We will come back to it. Essentially, it is only in circumstances where the claim is *justified* that costs can be claimed. If it was only ever a Small Claims Track case, then costs should only be paid on that basis.

Where does the LOC come from?

Many landlords are mystified why their tenants are instructing solicitors who practice hundreds of miles away from the tenants they represent. The answer is the claims management industry is responsible for generating the vast majority of disrepair claims, in my experience. This is 'ambulance chasing', but the victim does not move so is much easier to find.

Letters of Claim arrive in seemingly random numbers, often without any warning from the tenant themselves that they are unhappy. In cases outside London, they are usually sent by solicitors practising in the North of England, who in my experience bring the majority of housing disrepair claims throughout the country. Those firms are often or have been involved in personal injury claims. They are also pursuing Japanese Knotweed and Data Protection claims.

Most LOC are hopelessly vague and unspecific in one or more respects.

At an early stage in the litigation, landlords need to identify the merits of any claim, and the areas in which the LOC is plainly wrong.

Taking the LOC as a structure to identify the areas which need investigation provides as good a springboard as any in looking at how to respond to claims.

The origin of most disrepair claims

In my experience, most disrepair claims are generated by Claims Management Companies, although solicitors do advertise themselves to generate business. Although figures for disrepair claims are not available, Aviva, the insurer, said generally of cold calls and texts in November 2019:

> *"Aviva's research found that consumers were targeted with 996 million nuisance calls and texts relating specifically to an injury-related claim (such as whiplash, holiday sickness, etc.), pension, PPI or other financial service-related claims, which translates to 2,728,767 calls and texts per day, or 1,895 made every minute. These calls account for nearly one in four (23.2%) of all cold calls in the UK."*

A substantial proportion of tenants who have instructed these solicitors will have answered an advert on Facebook, received a leaflet in a shopping centre or similar, or answered a knock at their front door, a call on their telephone or a text.

The Conduct of Authorised Persons Rules 2014, in rule 4 of the Client Specific Rules, bans cold calling and restricts other marketing in relation to conditional fee claims:

> *"Cold calling in person is prohibited. Any marketing by telephone, email, fax or text shall be inaccordance with the Direct Marketing Association's Code and any related guidance issued by the Direct Marketing Association."*

So Claims Management Companies should not be recruiting tenants with aggressive marketing, but they seem to do so.

Basics of the Protocol

The Pre-Action Protocol for Housing Conditions sets out the steps which should be taken in the absence of exceptional circumstances when a tenant wishes to sue their landlord for disrepair.

The Protocol gives a roadmap to solicitors, enabling them even as beginners in landlord and tenant law to plan how they should bring a claim. It provides a structure, showing them how to prepare to sue, what evidence to collect and how to rely on it. It therefore repays careful study.

Some solicitors do not seem to know much more than what is in the Protocol and what they have learned along the way. Nor do many surveyors instructed on behalf of claimants seem to know the law behind the physical condition of the building and what satisfies the threshold test of "disrepair" or "unfitness".

So, it is up to a landlord to be questioning and to challenge any assertion by outsiders that their repairs and maintenance policies are deficient. But doing so is often extremely challenging. Lack of specificity in the LOC often means that it is difficult to know what real merit there is in any claim.

Requests for claimant solicitors to tie their claim down are met with obfuscation and further generalities. This is often because it is not possible to be more specific, as the tenant does not know any more than what is in the LOC. Rarely, this might be because the tenant really has complained but has genuinely forgotten. More often it is because only a small part of the allegations are true. We will look at how to discover whether this is so in your case.

Letters of Claim are open to challenge

An LOC can look daunting to the uninitiated. With the various documents mandated by the Protocol attached, the letter can run to 20 pages and more. It may be that there is no intention to cause consternation, but landlords receiving such seemingly detailed correspondence might well be somewhat overwhelmed.

Although on careful analysis, there will be usually be some merit in one or more of the allegations in the letter of claim, they are frequently overstated and/or unsupported by the contemporaneous records. Usually, the allegations are so general and so wide-ranging that, at first sight, it appears that the landlord has simply handed the keys to the tenant at the start of the tenancy and walked away, allowing their property to crumble while they spend the rent on anything but property maintenance.

Although the onus should be on the tenant to be specific from the outset about the real nature of any genuine complaint they have, it is almost invariably left to the landlord to attempt to whittle the claim down. Investigations must either discover what was actually complained of, and when, or sometimes establish that the tenant is not truly unhappy with the repairs process but had been promised some compensation and has taken advantage of the offer made by their solicitors to obtain it.

What should be challenged?

It follows that claims need to be approached with a sceptical but open mind. Thought needs to be given to every aspect of the allegations. Genuine claims need to be identified at the earliest possible moment, so that realistic offers of works and compensation can be made before costs escalate to even more unacceptable levels. More about the high costs generated in these cases later, but most landlords will be familiar with the surprising figures claimed for costs even in cases settled shortly after inception.

Chapter Summary/Key Takeaways

- The LOC can be used as a template from which to examine and respond to disrepair claims.

- Letters of Claim should not be taken at face value. They may contain allegations which on investigation are not borne out on the facts of the case.

- In the next chapter we will consider the various headings of the LOC as a whole and before looking at each of them individually.

CHAPTER THREE

THE LETTER OF CLAIM
AS A GUIDE

The LOC can form the basis of an investigation into the claim, a checklist of what needs to be researched and determined before a decision is made whether to contest it or to concede, and if so what works to do and how much to offer in compensation.

But it is important to bear in mind that this assessment should not be carried out by lawyers, but within the internal complaints process. An understanding of the LOC is essential to justify that statement.

The Contents of the Letter of Claim

The content of a LOC is mandated by the Pre-Protocol in Annex A of the Pre-Action Protocol. The Appendix of the Pre-Action Protocol for Housing Conditions contains an example standard LOC. While it is not prescriptive, the form of the LOC in the Annex is almost invariably slavishly copied, although the details are usually woefully lacking in certain respects.

The Protocol requires the following information to be included in the LOC, which I will use in the following chapters to explore how to respond to a claim.

An Explicit Reliance on the Pre-Action Protocol

The letter begins by making a statement which is more often honoured in the breach, in my experience. It states that the tenant's solicitors are using the Protocol. This is about avoiding litigation except where absolutely necessary.

But usually, tenant solicitors do not adhere properly to spirit of the Protocol. The Protocol contains some fundamental restrictions on its use, in its Introduction and its early paragraphs.

First, it says that it should only be used in cases where the tenant has "*ensured*" that their *landlord is aware* of the poor housing conditions relied upon in support of the claim. In theory this should mean that the solicitors have asked their client for proof that they have complained that works have not been done despite being told about problems.

Second, the fundamental stated aim of the Protocol is to "*avoid unnecessary litigation*". The Protocol says this can be achieved by the use of alternative dispute resolution. For social housing tenants this expressly includes the landlord's internal complaints process.

Therefore the first part of our investigation will involve looking at how the above restrictions should affect the instruction of lawyers by tenants to pursue landlords and on when it is appropriate to follow the majority of the Protocol at all, as ADR should avoid the need for doing so.

Details of the tenant

The letter should give details of the name and address of the tenant and their property. Sometimes these details are incorrect, either in naming the wrong tenant, or omitting a joint tenant.

Defects alleged

The letter should follow with a description of the defects and may include a schedule showing each of the defects alleged, room by room. They rarely do include that schedule.

History of each defect

The letter should describe the history of each defect in turn. Usually they do not do so.

Notice

It should say when notice was given, in list form. This detail is often fundamental and is rarely provided in sufficient detail for the landlord to check their files against the allegaitons.

Effects of the defects

Details should be provided of the effects on the tenant and their family, individually, listing any personal injury alleged to be suffered. The Solicitors are required to specify whether there will be any additional claimants. If other potential claims are not mentioned at this point, the landlord can later get a nasty surprise.

Provision for inspection

The LOC should state that the landlord needs to inspect as soon as possible, provide dates and times for access in list form.

Confirmation whether works intended

The landlord should be asked to provide confirmation whether they intend to carry out remedial works immediately or to wait for expert inspection.

Schedule of intended works

If the landlord is intending to carry out works, it should ask for a full schedule of those works and anticipated start and completion dates, with a timetable. My approach does not include the provision of a response to this question by lawyers, but by the complaints team.

Disclosure

The LOC will request disclosure of relevant documents, and should provide copies of relevant documents from the tenant, but never does so. A Form of Authority must be included to allow the landlord to disclose such documents. Again, for reasons I will address, at an early stage disclosure to lawyers of all the documents listed in the Protocol is unnecessary and should be resisted.

Expert Evidence

The letter should say that a Single Joint Expert Surveyor will be instructed on behalf of the claimant if agreement is not reached about the carrying out of works within 20 working days of the letter, upon which the letter should propose a joint instruction. It should enclose a CV and draft letter of instruction. It should invite any objections within 20 working days. If the landlord wants to send their own instructions, they are asked to send them directly to the expert within 20 working days and provide a copy to the landlord.

If agreement is not reached as to the instruction of an SJE, the letter will propose instruction of an expert to inspect in any event. They should invite a joint inspection.

Again, at this stage, no external, independent expert should be inspecting the property, for reasons I will discuss.

Details of the damages and injunction claim

The LOC should conclude with an assertion that there has been a breach of repairing obligations and a request for proposals for compensation, or a suggestion as to general damages, with details of any special damages sought.

General approach of the book

We are going to take the LOC apart from beginning to end, to plan how to respond to it. The response to an LOC might not simply be to that particular claim itself – it might involve changing maintenance and improvement policies and procedures.

ADR before going through the Protocol steps

We will start with the question whether it is necessary to follow through all the steps of the Protocol on receipt of the LOC. I believe that the parties should attempt ADR before progressing with it.

I am delighted that at lest one judge in the Court of Appeal now agrees with me (hopefully you have read the Preface and know about the decision in *Hockett v Bristol City Council*).

More of this later but start thinking about it now.

Chapter Summary/Key Takeaways

- From the point of view of solicitors working for tenants, the Letter of Claim contains the building blocks of the case against a landlord. It often overlooks the first and fundamental question, whether they should be incurring legal costs at all.

- The LOC is often deficient in one or more respects. However, given that in many cases it should not even have been written at this stage in the life of a complaint about living conditions, that may not be an issue.

- Tenant solicitors do not approve of the use of the landlord's internal complaints procedure, as it obviates the need for lawyers to be involved.

- Complaints procedures should provide a free, quick and efficient way to deal with dissatisfaction with housing conditions

- Therefore, the first part of this book looks at whether the tenant should be using Alternative Dispute Resolution ("ADR") instead of instructing solicitors to pursue their landlord.

- If ADR fails, the LOC then should also form the basis of the landlord's investigation whether the claim should be fought or settled-, whether works should be done and compensation offered.

- In the following chapters we will look at the rationale behind the LOC, then move to an analysis of the facts on which the claim is based. It is important to understand the opening parts of the Protocol, because most claimant solicitors completely ignore them.

So first, ADR.

PART III

THE PRE-ACTION PROTOCOL AND ALTERNATIVE DISPUTE RESOLUTION

It is essential to do everything possible to obviate the need for a legal claim. This is entirely possible if the Pre-Action Protocol is followed properly.

Claimant solicitors do not like this approach, as they should not be involved in it where social housing is concerned.

My approach, which has mostly succeeded for years, is to insist on compliance with the letter and spirit of the Protocol, in its reference to ADR and in particular to the landlord's internal complaints procedure.

I am repeating this point as it demands a shift in the way most social landlords respond to these claims.

In this part of the book I will explain how and why it succeeds in reducing unnecessary disrepair claims and saving costs, which can then be spent on repairs, to the benefit of everyone involved in social housing, except lawyers.

CHAPTER FOUR

THE FUNDAMENTAL IMPORTANCE OF THE PRE-ACTION PROTOCOL

As I have said, the LOC will begin with a statement that the tenant's solicitors are using the Protocol. This is often true only in part, because they do not adhere properly to the Protocol and use it only so far as it suits them. The Protocol assumes that tenant solicitors will only pursue claims for defects which do amount to a claim in law.

When read carefully, the Protocol contains some clear restrictions on its use, in its Introduction and in its early paragraphs it stresses the importance of avoiding legal claims if at all possible.

For social landlords, that specifically allows them to avoid the unnecessary use of lawyers. To understand why this should be so, it is necessary to look at the origins of the Protocol and the competing interests of those who drafted it.

In this chapter we will look at paragraphs 1, 2 and 3 of the Protocol, because they lead onto a consideration of the fourth and most important paragraph. You can use paragraph 4 to head off claims before they become a legal nightmare.

Paragraph 1 is the Introduction. Paragraph 2 states the aims. Paragraph 3 states the Scope of the Protocol. In this chapter we will look briefly at each of those paragraphs.

Paragraph 1: The Introduction

The Introduction contains four central principles:

- the tenant must **ensure their landlord is aware of the poor housing conditions of which they complain**

- the Protocol sets out the **conduct which the court will** "*normally expect prospective parties in a claim to engage in*"

- if the claim proceeds to court, **the judge will expect all parties to have complied with the Protocol** "*as far as possible*".

- In the event of a failure by one party to comply, **the court can order a party in breach either to pay costs** "*or to be subject to other sanctions*".

Those four fundamental principles can give rise to significant argument about how the Protocol should be applied by tenant solicitors. It is easy to understand why the first of the statements concerns whether the landlord knows of the problems which the tenant is experiencing.

Fundamental requirement in the PAP that the landlord should be on notice

In its first paragraph, it says "***Before using** the Protocol, tenants should ensure that their landlord is aware of (their poor housing) conditions. **The Protocol is intended for those cases where, despite the landlord's knowledge of the poor conditions, matters remain unresolved.**"

This is often the first issue in housing disrepair claims. Landlords are surprised to receive a LOC from a claimant tenant's solicitors. They check their records and find that there are no outstanding complaints that repairs have not been carried out.

Alternatively, although a landlord might be aware of one or two of the defects in the LOC, most of them will not have been brought to their attention. They often express surprise to the solicitors that the claim has been threatened, but, in my experience, rarely do anything about the lack of notice.

We will look at notice in more detail in Chapter 5.

Paragraph 2: The Stated Aims of the Protocol-ADR is central

In its second paragraph of the Protocol specifically states that its first aim is to "avoid unnecessary litigation". It then lists others, which we will address in other chapters. The sixth aim is to "*keep the costs of resolving disputes down*".

As you are likely to know, tenant solicitors using the Protocol who succeed in extracting a promise to do works and a small payment of compensation often then produce a costs schedule for the landlord. Usually they claimbetween £5,000 and £10,000, a totally disproportionate amount measured against the value of the works and the agreed compensation. Thus in many cases, when it is not applied properly, the Protocol fails in its fundamental aim.

ADR is therefore central to the aims of the Protocol. If the landlord and the tenant themselves both engage in it properly, in most cases there should be no need for lawyers to be instructed. We will return to this aspect when we have looked at when the Protocol will apply and when parties can ignore it, in Chapter 8.

Paragraph 3: The Scope of the Protocol

Paragraph 3 of the Protocol describes when the Protocol should and should not be used. First, although the Protocol must be used in most disrepair claims, there are some circumstances in which it is not relevant, in particular when a counterclaim is made in possession or other proceedings against the tenant. That deserves separate consideration, in the next chapter.

Paragraph 3 sets out the circumstances in which parties *must* use the Protocol. If someone is making a personal injury claim which arises as a result of a failure to repair, or the defective state of premises, the Protocol will be relevant. However, just to complicate matters, if an injury claim needs medical evidence other than a GP's letter, the claimant solicitors have to follow the Personal Injury Protocol, but only in respect of that element of the claim.

Also, if a disrepair claim is urgent, solicitors are allowed to bring separate disrepair and personal-injury claims, which might then be case-managed together or consolidated. But provided the disrepair claim is truly urgent, a landlord would be liable for the costs of both and could not argue that

31

the latter was unnecessary. Such situations should be very rare for social landlords.

The Protocol should also be used when people other than tenants make such claims, for instance sub- tenants and members of the tenant's family.

Unwary landlords can be caught out by dealing with claims in respect of a tenant, only to receive separate and additional claims from others living in the property. If settling a claim, care should be taken to ensure that any other possible claimants are included in the terms of the settlement agreement.

Previously most claims were pursued primarily under section 11 of the Landlord and Tenant Act 1985 and under the covenants in the tenancy. Claims are now also made relying on section 9A that Act. The Protocol also covers claims brought under the various other forms of legal remedy available to occupants-the Defective Premises Act 1972, claims in common law nuisance and negligence, etc.

The LTA 1985 and its amended provisions under section 9 will only apply to tenancies of less than seven years, all existing periodic tenancies and new and assured tenancies with a fixed term of seven years or more. Also if the landlord of a longer letting is able to terminate the tenancy within seven years of its start date, the 1985 Act will apply.

If you are dealing with anything other than a standard periodic assured or secure tenancy, it pays to give consideration as to whether it will be excluded from the provisions of the Act. It is rare to come across a residential lease for a term in excess of a few years, or under about 40 years in London and 100 years elsewhere, so most people making these claims will be able to rely on the implied terms of the 1985 Act.

The Protocol is not relevant where a claim is brought under section 82 of the Environmental Protection Act 1990. They are dealt with in the Magistrates' Court.

The Protocol should be used whatever the value of the claim-thus even if it is only a small claim, the parties are obliged to follow it. In my view that makes ADR all the more important.

Chapter Summary/Key Takeaways

- The terms of the Protocol should dictate the manner in which a landlord is alerted to disrepair problems, and how they respond to that notification.

- The stated aim of the Protocol is to keep costs of litigation down, by avoiding unnecessary litigation.

- The scope of the Protocol is unlikely to be an issue in most cases received by landlords, but it is worth thinking about how its principles might be applied, e.g. in counterclaims.

- Because the issue of notice is so fundamental to disrepair claims, the following chapter looks in detail at the questions of when notice is not required and the exceptions to that rule, before we look at the question of notice as set out in the Protocol.

CHAPTER FIVE

WHEN IS NOTICE NOT REQUIRED?

Notice is a fundamental battleground in disrepair claims. You will need a thorough understanding of the legal principles behind the question. We are looking at it now because a landlord will not be liable for any significant damages for loss of amenity unless the tenant can prove that they were aware of a defect and it was not addressed within a reasonable time.

You might refer to two books in particular, as mentioned in the Introduction. First, for a more concise consideration, "Housing Conditions, tenants' rights", by HHJ Jan Luba QC, Catherine O'Donnell and Giles Peaker, and for a more in-depth study, "Dilapidations, The Modern Law and Practice" by Dowding & Reynolds.

You should be able to cite both in court in argument to support your case. It is important to recognise situations in which the tenant may argue that the landlord is liable even though they have not had notice of the defect. The reason that this surprising principle exists lies in the ability of the tenant to know of the defect.

Notice is important whether the defect does amount to disrepair, renders the property unfit for human habitation or is merely something which the landlord will usually address within its service criteria despite the fact it has no legal duty to do so. This is because in the landlord's formal Complaints Procedure, compensation might be payable for a service failure as well as a breach of legal duty. We will look at that principle later.

The law in respect of notice is tricky and sometimes counterintuitive so you need to understand the subtleties.

When a tenant is not expected to notify the landlord of a defect

In some circumstances a tenant cannot be expected to know of a defect and therefore they cannot be expected to report it. So, in those situations, the landlord is said to be liable to repair the defect from the date on which it arises. That is not a problem, but if a tenant then claims damages for a period during which the landlord was not in fact aware of a defect, the rule might seem unfair. But it is limited in its application.

When the defect is not in the demised property

When there is a defect which is outside the demised property, the tenant can rely on a principle of law that the landlord's liability arises when the defect occurs, even if the landlord is not aware of the defect. No notice is required when the landlord has possession and control of that area. For instance, if a dead pigeon blocks a downfall overflow pipe above a flat and causes a flood which damages the tenant's furniture, that defect gives rise to liability[1].

The rationale of the principle is that the requirement of notice in cases where a defect is in the demised property itself is really an exception to the general principle that a landlord who covenants to keep a property in repair agrees to do so at all times, so effectively it is the landlord's problem when there is any defect.

Of course, a landlord with a repairing covenant should be liable to repair, for example, both a defect in the roof of a block of flats and the immediate damage caused to the property when it manifests itself in a flat below.

But in housing disrepair, the claimant's solicitors may seek to apply the principle to damages for loss of amenity over a period of years, despite the fact their client has not reported the water ingress. Alternatively, the claimant might have reported it some years previously, but was out when

---

[1] *Bishop v Consolidated London Properties Ltd* (1933) 102 LJ KB 257; *Minchburn v Peck* (1987) 20 HLR 392, *BT plc v Sun Life* [1996] Ch 69 and other cases-see Dowding & Reynolds at 22-16

the repairs team attended to inspect and did not rearrange the appointment.

Although the general rule is clear, fortunately there are several exceptions and the rule that a claimant must mitigate their loss can also help the landlord.

Where the defect is caused by an occurrence wholly outside the landlord's control

In the *BT v Sun Life* case, the court did not express any concluded view about cases where damage occurs which is entirely outside the landlord's control. The examples given was roof damage caused by a branch falling from a tree standing on a neighbouring property outside the landlord's control. Provisionally the judge said that he could not see any reason why that case should not be a further exception to the general rule. In theory tenants should be insured against that sort of occurrence.

That exception is limited to events which originate on land in the possession and control of a third-party. Where an unforeseeable defect arises on the landlord's property[2] the exception will not be applied. In another case[3] Hobhouse LJ doubted that it is relevant that the defect was outside the landlord's control, saying that it is only when the landlord or the tenant is responsible for the defect that causation becomes relevant. In that case, a frozen pipe burst and caused damage. The court held in the event that this was not an event which was wholly outside the landlord's control, because frozen pipes are not uncommon in this country. Landlords should take preventative measures such as insulating them.

The lease may require notice before liability to repair arises

But some leases may provide that the landlord's duty to repair only arises upon the giving of notice. Generally, provided a covenant to that effect is clear enough, the courts will uphold it and the landlord is not under

---

[2] as in *Bavage v Southwark LBC* [1998] C LY 3623

[3] *Passley v Wandsworth LBC* (1998) 30 HLR 165

any obligation to repair until the tenant informs them of the damage to their flat and, therefore, by inference, of a defect in the structure.

In such a case[4] the landlord will not be liable for the initial damage, unless they fail to repair within the time stipulated in the tenancy, but even then should only be liable for damages for loss of amenity rather than the original effect of (say) a flood caused by a roof defect. This might seem unfair on the tenant, but household insurance is designed for such eventualities.

But in housing disrepair claims, it has been argued successfully at first instance that section 12 of the 1985 Act prevents a landlord from requiring a tenant to give notice of disrepair before liability to repair arises, as the section prevents a landlord from contracting out of their duties. That principle has yet to be tested on appeal. In this context, there is a difference between the liability to repair and liability to pay general damages for loss of amenity during the period prior to the tenant giving notice of damage to their flat.

The covenant has the potential to operate unfairly to a landlord

it is clear that the rule has the potential to operate unfairly against the landlord if misapplied. Take an example where there is a roof leak in a building where there is no access to the roof (except e.g., by scaffolding), or there are pinprick defects in a flat roof surface Invisible to the naked eye. Water ingress through the ceiling occurs in a flat but the tenant fails to report it for a period of years.

That would cause the tenant knowingly and voluntarily to suffer any loss of amenity caused by the water penetration. If this principle is applied without any further analysis, the landlord might appear to be liable for that loss of amenity even though they had no idea that the roof was in disrepair. If, for instance, the tenant is not using a room or they are absent from the flat for long periods, they could deliberately accrue a claim for damages against an unsuspecting landlord.

---

[4] e.g. as in a New Zealand case, *Masterton Licensing Trust v Finco* [1957] NZLR 1137

The tenant has failed to mitigate the damage they suffer

In such a case, the tenant who fails to notify their landlord of water penetration and therefore suffers continuing loss of amenity fails to mitigate the damage which they are suffering[5].

Although they will be able to insist on the landlord repairing the roof leak and any damage to plaster, furniture and decorations caused by the initial flood, there is no good reason that they should recover damages for any loss suffered as a result of their deliberate silence after they first noticed the damp penetration.

Damages are likely to be significantly lower where there has been a failure to mitigate. The difference between liability for the initial damage and for the damage suffered after a failure to report could be very substantial. If a tenant notices a few drips coming through his ceiling and reports it immediately, the leak might be fixed before they suffer any significant loss of amenity and before any decorations, floor coverings and furniture are damaged.

But if the tenant says nothing about it until years later, they might claim substantial damages for loss of amenity. They should not be awarded them for the period during which they did not complain, because they have entirely failed to mitigate their loss. They are entitled to insist the landlord repairs the defect, but only to damages perhaps reflecting minor staining to the decorations which would have remedied much sooner had they reported the defect. Further, it is arguable that the landlord should counterlaim against the tenant for the additional damage caused by their act of waste.

Thus the principle that notice is not always necessary, unfair though it looks at first sight, can operate fairly if applied properly.

---

[5] see *Minchburn v Peck*, above, and para 22-22 and 33-37 in Dowding & Reynolds (although the Court only reduced damages by 10%, for reasons unknown)

Blocks of flats subject to the statutory consultation procedure

The rule might also be prejudicial to a landlord who has to consult tenants before incurring maintenance costs chargeable underwritten by service charges. If the landlord's repairs cannot be started before carrying out the consultation procedure under section 20 and 20 ZA of the 1985 Act, and the landlord cannot afford to repair without receiving interim service charges, they may be liable in damages for loss of amenity even though they could not possibly have started the repairs.

But the consultation procedure is subject to an exception for emergency or urgent works. Also the lease might be expressly subject to contribution and payment by the lessee of the service charges necessary to fund the works. In another case,[6] Carnwath LJ suggested that the court might have to consider whether the rule in *BT v Sun Life* "*requires some modification to take into account the practicalities of the modern relationship of residential lessors and lessees*".

Where the defect arises in an area of the building in the possession of another tenant

In such a case, it seems that there are two possible scenarios.

First, where the tenant in a flat above a claimant commits some deliberate or negligent act which causes damage below, e.g. allows their bath to overflow and the resulting flood into the flat below causes damage. Provided there is nothing wrong with the installation for the supply of water or the intervening structure which allows the flood to descend, then that cause appears to be wholly outside the landlord's control. Again, it is the sort of event against which an insurance policy should be obtained. Of course the landlord would still have to repair the damage to the structure, but may be able to recover from the other tenant.

Alternatively if a pipe only bursts because the tenant above has gone on holiday and left the windows open during the winter, again the landlord might escape liability because, apart from making tenants aware of the

---

[6] *Earle v Charalambous* [2007] HLR 8

risks of freezing pipes and taking reasonable precautions to insulate exposed pipework, it is difficult to see why liability should arise.

But if a pipe bursts, the landlord may be liable. That might occur because of faulty plumbing, even years before, which left a hidden weakness in the pipe system. A landlord should be responsible for the damage which that causes.

Again that exception must be subject to the principle that the landlord would become liable for any loss of amenity suffered after they receive notice if they do not then remedy the defect in the neighbouring property within a reasonable period of time.

Chapter summary/key takeaways

- The issue of when notice is not required will confound many. The principles do not seem to be entirely fair, but there is a logic to them.

- The guidance above has scratched the surface of the issue and should provide some useful point of argument.

- In the next chapter we look at what the Protocol says about the tenant's duty to give notice and the implications for a claim.

CHAPTER SIX

THE PROTOCOL REQUIRES
A CLAIMANT TO GIVE
DETAILS OF NOTICE

The Protocol itself does not address the principle that notice of disrepair may not be necessary before liability to repair arises. As you will have gathered from the previous chapter, there is good reason for this omission.

As discussed in the last chapter, although a landlord might be liable to repair a defect even though they have not actually had notice, in principle a tenant should not recover damages for loss of amenity unless they have given their landlord notice of the fact that they are suffering such damage. Whenever there is penetrating damp, there is never is any dispute that a landlord is required to carry out repairs, e.g. to a roof of the block of flats in which a leak is occurring in someone's home below.

Therefore, the Protocol says that a defect which is affecting a tenant should not give rise to liability, at least under the Protocol, until the landlord is aware of it. Further, in any event most tenancies will contain a clause requiring the tenant to report disrepair, so it amounts to the same thing, whether it is a breach of contract by the tenant preventing liability for consequential damages from arising, or a total failure to mitigate.

Insisting on compliance with the Protocol

So my starting point in housing disrepair claims is based upon the premise that the Protocol is there to be observed properly by both parties, in respect of all of its provisions, not simply those on which claimant solicitors choose to rely. The tenant must prove notice and further give the landlord a reasonable period of time in which to effect a repair before going through the steps in the Protocol.

This approach is very unpopular with claimant solicitors, some of whom appear to believe that they are entitled to ignore the express words of the Protocol when it does not suit them.

The first response to the LOC – when notice not given

it follows that, in the reply to the LOC, if the tenant has not previously complained that repairs are not being carried out, landlords should refer to this paragraph of the Protocol first. They should say that the tenant should not be using the Protocol in cases where the landlord was not aware of the defects. For this reason, the landlord should not respond to the LOC with a reply within the Protocol but treat it as notification from a tenant of the existence of a repairable defect.

That means the landlord is entitled to take the LOC as 'notice' and respond to it outside the Protocol. If the tenant then goes ahead and issues proceedings, the landlord is entitled to say that this is a breach of the Protocol and should be the subject of sanctions. We will address those below.

Therefore, in cases where there is no notice of disrepair at all, the fundamental approach is to stop the further use of the Protocol, while the initial notice of defects given by the LOC is investigated by the landlord.

Such an approach will be met with protest from the tenant's solicitors, who may attempt to continue reliance on the Protocol, and then to issue proceedings. However, by that point, if a landlord has an efficient repairs service, works will have been carried out.

Access injunctions

If the tenant refuses to allow contractors in to carry out work, an application for an access injunction can be made. It will follow that a tenant cannot then claim specific performance of the repairing covenant on the grounds that a landlord is refusing to repair.

Unjustified claims for injunctions for specific performance

If the claimant does then include a claim for an injunction in any claim, the landlord should apply for summary judgement against the claimant on that part of the claim.

Treating the receipt of the LOC as the receipt of a complaint

As an alternative to this stance, rather than treating the receipt of the LOC as notice of a defect, in most cases the LOC can be treated as a complaint. The Protocol not only allows for that process to be followed; it mandates it. We turn to an investigation of how that is done in the context of cases where at least one defect was known of by the landlord.

Response to the LOC when notice has been given on one or more defects

In theory, in a case where a tenant has previously given notice of at least one of the defects on which the LOC relies, it is not as easy to respond by saying that the LOC is being taken as the first notice of the defects.

A landlord could approach the reply to the LOC on a hybrid basis, separating the defects relied on into those of which notice has been provided, or of which the landlord is or should be aware, and those which are entirely new. However, that would lead to such complexity that it is usually best to deal wholesale with the issues.

In practice this means instituting the internal Complaints Process, but keeping a clear distinction between defects of which there was previously notice, and those which were drawn to the attention of the landlord for the first time in the LOC.

In the case of defects where notice had been given, compensation might be payable for failure to carry out the works within a reasonable period and to a reasonable standard.

Otherwise, if notice had not been given of a defect but the Complaints Process finds that works are necessary, as long as they are done within a reasonable time, no compensation should be offered as there will have been no breach of duty.

Notice is fundamental to the defence of many claims

If the Complaints Process is unsuccessful in resolving the tenant's concerns and the tenant's solicitors pursue the claim, the arguments on notice will have to be raised as a defence to the claim in court.

Chapter Summary/Key Takeaways

- Often landlords do not appreciate the significance of the Introduction to the Protocol.

- Except in a few cases in which a tenant has complained of disrepair and nothing has been done, tenant solicitors always ignore the importance of the need to prove notice and a failure to repair as a precursor to writing the LOC.

- Upon receipt of the LOC, landlords often fail to use the content of the Protocol to respond appropriately to it. Many thousands of disrepair claims are started unnecessarily because both parties fail to follow the Protocol properly.

- Therefore, if a landlord is confident that they can prove that they have not received notice of any of the defects relied upon and liability does not arise without notice, they should carry out works pursuant to the notice they have received in the LOC and refuse to proceed with the remainder of the steps in the Protocol.

- If there was no constructive or actual knowledge on the part of the landlord, compensation for loss of amenity will not be payable. But if the tenant subsequently alleges that they are still unhappy with the standard or extent of repairs done, the Complaints Process should be instituted.

- In the next chapter we will look at counterclaims, when the Protocol need not be followed, and what can be done about the problem which that creates. Counterclaims for disrepair in rent proceedings areoften raised by tenants. Again, in most cases, the landlord is unaware of the impending disrepair counterclaim until they attend a possession hearing.

CHAPTER SEVEN

COUNTERCLAIMS
FOR DISREPAIR

Protocol need not be followed in some disrepair disputes

Landlords are accustomed to receiving counterclaims for disrepair in possession claims. The parties do not have to follow the Protocol in a counterclaim for disrepair. However, this does not mean that a tenant will necessarily be allowed to adjourn possession proceedings just because they bring a claim for disrepair.

For instance, a tenant may be accused of serious antisocial behaviour or may have substantial rent arrears. But when the parties attend for the first hearing (the CPR 55.8 Return Date), the landlord is surprised when the tenant's solicitor says that there is outstanding disrepair.

Occasionally there may be some merit in the allegation, or at least the defects might exist. There may be repairs which have not been carried out for a variety of reasons. Sometimes because the landlord has genuinely failed to comply with its obligations.

Surprise counterclaims

More often, a landlord consults its repairs records and finds that there is no mention of the defects relied upon in its systems. Alternatively, the tenant may have had some repairs done and the remedial works were not quite finished off or they were not done to a perfect standard. Again, often, on inspecting their records, they find there were no outstanding concerns concerning repairs.

A party who wishes to bring a counterclaim must comply with CPR 20.

Before the Defence is filed

The defendant does not need permission to file a counterclaim as long as it is done as part of their Defence. In counterclaims, it is worth considering whether you can proceed with the possession claim with an order for a split trial despite the fact that the counterclaim has been raised.

Such an order might be appropriate where there has been serious antisocial behaviour and the counterclaim could be pursued whether or not the tenant remains in possession. Equally, if rent arrears are very substantial and the disrepair is objectively modest, you may be able to argue that there is clearly no defence to the majority of the rent claim and therefore a possession order should be made, although possibly suspended depending on quantum.

However if a counterclaim is drafted at any other time, the defendant must apply for permission (CPR 20.4 (2) (b)). If pursued late in the day, you should consider whether to object and to ask that the possession claim be tried immediately, without an adjournment to provide for the disrepair claim to be heard at the same hearing.

Imposing terms on the grant of permission to pursue a counterclaim

In both cases, the landlord should argue that, although the counterclaim should proceed, or the court might give permission to pursue a disrepair counterclaim, permission to pursue the counterclaim should be conditional upon the tenant making interim payments of rent and arrears, with a provision that a possession order should be made if the tenant fails to keep up their payments. Alternatively, if there have been problems with access, they can be addressed by way of undertaking or injunction.

Systems to prevent surprise counterclaims

Given the number of claims in which an ambush disrepair defence is raised, it is worth thinking about how to pre-empt such delaying tactics. A landlord might introduce a system when considering whether to bring a possession claim to provide a complete answer to an attempted counterclaim. If the landlord already makes personal visits or requires an interview when contemplating eviction, there should be a mandatory requirement for the officer or employee concerned to ask in detail about the condition of the property.

The tenant should be asked specifically whether they have any concerns about the condition of their home, and the answer must be recorded in sufficient detail to render it credible. Thenif the tenant later raises it in the possession claim, the landlord will already have documentary proof that the issues were notpreviously mentioned.

Application for summary judgement on the counterclaim / a split trial

Although the court will be reluctant to separate the question of possession from a counterclaim for disrepair, in certain circumstances, if a landlord's evidence is good enough, the court might be prepared to make a possession order and adjourn the counterclaim for disrepair to be dealt with separately.

This is particularly pertinent if arrears are very high compared to the possible value of any counterclaim, or if there are allegations of antisocial behaviour. In the latter case it may be better to apply for a split trial of the ASB allegations before dealing with the disrepair claim.

In many cases an application for summary judgement against the counterclaiming defendant can be made. Often the records show that prior to the issue of proceedings there was no substantial dissatisfaction on the part of the tenant and therefore, even if there are defects in the property, the landlord did not have notice of them. Obviously in such a case it would be necessary to show that the landlord has completed any necessary works within a reasonable time after notification.

Applications for summary judgement against disrepair claimants form part of the process of defending claims anyway, so I will look at this area in more detail later in the book.

There are statutory restrictions against bringing possession proceedings where there is outstanding disrepair, but in my experience, those circumstances never arise in social housing, so it is not worth addressing them here.

Damages claims after a possession order

A defendant tenant might even ask for the permission of the court to make a counterclaim after a possession order has been made,[7] although a landlord will be alive to a possible abuse of process in respect of any claim which is not raised at the earliest possible stage in the proceedings, particularly where a tenant has been legally represented.

The case law is not very helpful to landlords on the point though and it is usually better to press for an early trial/summary dismissal of the counterclaim.

Chapter summary/key takeaways

- The scope of the Protocol is wide, but usually a landlord is not able to deflect a counterclaim for disrepair by requiring a tenant to go through it before pursuing a counterclaim.

- Instead, there are other ways of addressing a counterclaim brought as a tactical defence. The most fruitful approach is likely to be an application for a split trial or an application for summary judgement on the counterclaim. For those applications, the landlord needs excellent records and a clear approach to the issues raised by the tenant.

- But this chapter has been a divergence from the more usual circumstances of a disrepair claim.In the next chapter we look at how to get the court to apply the Protocol properly, through the use of ADR.

---

[7] *Rahman v Sterling Credit Ltd* [2001] 1 WLR 496 and *Midland Heart Ltd v Idawah* [2014] EW Misc B48 (11 July 2014)

CHAPTER EIGHT

ALTERNATIVE DISPUTE RESOLUTION

In most cases, when an LOC is received, even if the landlord was on notice, they were not aware that the tenant was allegedly unhappy with the repairs process, or at least unhappy enough to contemplate a legal claim. The Protocol allows for this eventuality in its opening paragraphs. It provides that the parties must consider ADR. This reflects the whole tone of the Civil Procedure Rules. It is one of the fundamental tenets of the 'overriding objective '.

In this chapter we will consider how the CPR, the Pre-Action Protocol for Housing Conditions and the Practice Direction relating to the Protocols fit together to make a compelling case for pre-litigation ADR through use of the landlord's complaints process. The notes in the White Book Volume 1 (at C1A-004) are very helpful if you are preparing a submission to the court on the subject of ADR, as is section 14 in Volume 2 on ADR.

We will look separately at the law behind mandatory ADR in the chapter on summary judgement/strike out/stay applications.

The CPR are very clear in their aim of discouraging unnecessary litigation.

The Overriding Objective

The fundamental principle of the Rules is that they enable the court to deal with cases justly and at proportionate cost (CPR 1.1 (1). That includes, so far as is possible, the factors set out in sub-paragraph (2), all of which are relevant to the question whether ADR should be attempted before proceedings are allowed to continue.

By CPR 1.2 the court is obliged to give effect to the overriding objective in exercising powers given to it under the rules, or in interpreting them.

Finally, the parties are required by CPR 1.3 to help the court to further the overriding objective. This specifically means that the court should weigh up the proportionality of allowing a case to go to trial rather than staying it for ADR.

Asking the court to case manage the claim toward ADR

The court's duty to further the overriding objective is carried out by active case management, including, in CPR 1.4 (2) (a), encouraging the parties to cooperate with each other in the conduct proceedings, and in subparagraph (e), encouraging the parties to use an alternative dispute resolution if the court considers that appropriate and facilitating the use of such procedure, and in subparagraph (f), helping the parties to settle the whole or part of the case.

This is supported by the provisions of CPR 3.1, which gives the court the power to impose sanctions failing to engage in ADR when read with the Practice Direction to the Protocols:

- CPR 3.1 (2) (f) provides similarly that the court may: *"stay the whole or part of any proceedings... either generally or until a specified date or event"*;

- CPR 3.1 (4) provides *"Where the court gives directions it will take into account whether or not a party has complied with the Practice Direction (Pre-Action Conduct) and any relevant pre-action protocol"*.

Although the Court is specifically reminded by the CPR and PD of the ability to impose a sanction in costs, such a post-trial penalty is of limited benefit to a party which has had to spend substantial periods of time in the preparation of responses to disrepair claims. Further, most of the time the costs ordered against the unsuccessful tenant are much lower than those incurred.

The various Pre-Action Protocols provide for differing methods of alternative dispute resolution depending on the nature of the parties. In housing disrepair litigation, many cases involve social housing landlords and their tenants. Those organisations are likely to have a formal complaints process which is available for use by tenants at nil cost and in which it is not necessary to instruct lawyers on either side.

The Requirement to Consider ADR in Paragraph 4.1 of the Pre-Action Protocol

Paragraph 4 of the Protocol for Housing Conditions concerns ADR.

By paragraph 4.1, the parties are required to *"consider whether some form of ADR procedure would be more suitable than litigation and if so, try to agree which form of ADR to use."*

Either party might *"be required by the court to provide evidence that alternative means of resolving their dispute were considered."*

It is fundamental to my approach to disrepair litigation that this paragraph is situated before provisions relating to the LOC and the landlord's reply.

It is legitimate for a landlord to request the tenant's solicitors' cooperation in avoiding litigation, including even the use of the Protocol. Read in conjunction with the Introduction, paragraph 1.1, this means that the lawyers' steps in the Protocol should not be pursued unless it is necessary because the landlord has failed, despite knowing about "poor conditions" to remedy them and attempts at ADR have failed.

Thought must be given as to whether ADR in general would be *"more suitable than litigation"*. What does that mean? Factors such as the landlord's approach to notice of defects, the urgency of the situation in terms of the amenity of the property and the financial position of the parties might be relevant. Clearly it is easy to make out a case that cost-free and speedy ADR would be more suitable than litigation.

Thus a landlord needs to alert the tenant's solicitors immediately to the requirement to *"consider"* ADR. While, as presently worded, the Protocol does not *mandate* the parties to attempt ADR, that may not always be the case in the future.

In the meantime, the "consideration" of ADR is policed only once proceedings have been issued and then only if a party raises an objection to the continuation of the claim based on a breach of the PAP.

We will now consider how this is done through reliance on provisions of the CPR and PDs.

The PD to the Pre-Action Protocols

The Introduction to the Practice Direction for Pre-Action Conduct and Protocols ("the PD") and early paragraphs of the PD are very important in disrepair litigation. The Introduction is helpful as it sets the tone of the approach which the court is expected to take to discouraging unnecessary litigation. It also sets out the manner in which the court can control the behaviour of the parties in respect of breaches of the Protocol.

The Practice Direction – requirement to consider ADR

In brief, the PD to the Protocols provides at:

- paragraph 8, that "*litigation should be a last resort.*"

- paragraph 11 that: "*If proceedings are issued, the parties may be required by the court to provide evidence that ADR has been considered. A party's silence in response to an invitation to participate or a refusal to participate in ADR might be considered unreasonable by the court and could lead to the court ordering that party to pay additional court costs.*"

Sanctions for refusing to consider ADR

This Introduction is supplemented by paragraphs 13, 14, 15 and 16.

- paragraph 13: "*If a dispute proceeds to litigation, the court will expect the parties to have complied with a relevant pre-action protocol or this Practice Direction. The court will take into account non-compliance when giving directions for the management of proceedings (see CPR 3.1 (4) to (6).... The court will consider whether all parties have complied in substance with the terms of the relevant pre-action protocol or this Practice Direction and is not*" *likely to be concerned with minor or technical infringements, especially when the matter is urgent (for example an application for an injunction)."*

- paragraph 14: *"the court may decide that there has been a failure of compliance when a party has … unreasonably refused to use a form of ADR…"*;

- Paragraph 15: *"where there has been non-compliance with a pre-action protocol or this Practice Direction, the court may order that:*

  o *the parties are relieved of the obligation to comply or further comply with the pre-action protocol or this Practice Direction;*

  o *the proceedings are stayed while particular steps are taken to comply with the pre-action protocol or this Practice Direction;*

  o *sanctions are to be applied."*

- Paragraph 16: *"the court will consider the effect of any non-compliance when deciding whether to impose any sanctions …"*

Thus, if a tenant refuses to engage in the Complaints Process under paragraph 4 of the Protocol, a landlord can argue that it is relieved of the obligation to comply or carry out the steps under paragraph 5 and 6 of the Protocol.

The tenant will then be at risk as to sanctions should they issue proceedings prematurely. But they are not prevented from litigating forever-their access to justice is not impeded, merely delayed for a short period while more proportionate means of resolving the dispute are attempted. I discuss these provisions in more detail below, although normally the decision of Bean, LJ in *Hockett v Bristol City Council* should now be enough to persuade an unwilling claimant solicitor to advise their client to exhaust the internal complaints process before going back to them.

Paragraph 13

Paragraph 13 says that the parties are expected to have complied with the relevant PAP, or the Practice Direction and, crucially that the court will *"take into account non-compliance when **giving directions for the management of the proceedings** (see CPR 3.1 (4) to (6)) **and** when making orders for costs (see CPR 44.3 (5) (a)).*

When raised at an early stage in the proceedings, this paragraph allows the court to make case management decisions which result from a failure to engage in ADR. Sanctions are not limited to costs at the end of the proceedings. Claimants rely on historic case law to assert that the court should not order a stay for ADR – but the new PAPs do not support that restrictive approach.

Paragraph 14

That is expressly provided for by paragraph 14 (c), which says that the court can decide there has been a failure of compliance if a party has *"unreasonably refused to use a form of ADR, or failed to respond at all to an invitation to do so."*

So there is a specific provision allowing the court to change the course of a case by making a case management decision based on a refusal to respond to an invitation to ADR or the unreasonable refusal of ADR.

Paragraph 15

Paragraph 15 then sets out what the court can do if there has been non-compliance with the Protocol or the PD.

Crucially, the court may order that by subparagraph (a) *"the parties are relieved of the obligation to comply or further comply"* with the PAP or PD. That means that a landlord might not be criticised for failing to respond in detail to the LOC under the PAP.

The court can also order that *"the proceedings are stayed while particular steps are taken to comply with the pre-action protocol or this Practice Direction".* Thus, the parties can be ordered to consider ADR properly.

Whether that can go beyond mere consideration is a moot point, to be argued in the near future.

Finally, paragraph 15 (c) allows the court to impose sanctions on a party who has unreasonably refused to use a form of ADR. Such sanctions might include costs, but in an appropriate case, the claim can be struck out or stayed for such refusal.

Paragraph 16

Paragraph 16 requires the court to consider the effect of any non-compliance when deciding whether to impose sanctions, which may *include* an order for costs of the whole or part of the proceedings on an indemnity basis, depriving a successful party of interest, or giving penalty interest to a successful party.

Arguing for a more effective sanction than costs for failure to use ADR

So although there is no specific sanction such as strike out mentioned in the Introduction, the court is not prevented from imposing such a serious penalty, as paragraph 16 gives *examples* of specific costs penalties only, rather than including every form of sanction.

It is necessary for the rules specifically to provide for those sanctions, because the normal order for costs after a successful claim is that the loser pays them. These provisions allow the court to depart from that rule. But the rule does not exclude other forms of sanction.

We have addressed paragraph 4.1 of the Protocol and the relevant paragraphs of the Introduction to the Practice Direction. We now turn to the type of ADR which is mandated in disrepair claims.

Paragraph 4.2 of the Protocol – ADR options

The first line of defence is that a landlord was unaware of the defects at all. If that does not apply, because there is evidence that they knew of any issue, or the defect has been investigated and dealt with but the tenant remains unhappy, we move on to how ADR can then be used despite the tenant instructing solicitors.

57

The Protocol provides specific options for resolving a dispute. In particular, for all tenants, mediation can be considered (paragraph 4.2 (a).

Private landlords may find this particularly useful and there are some free court mediation schemes. Also for private tenants, the Protocol provides in paragraph 4.2 (d) that *"the landlord, letting agent or property manager may be a member of a redress scheme enabling unresolved complaints about housing conditions to be independently resolved"*.

However a social landlord has a wider variety of ADR options open to it. Paragraph 4.2 (b) and (c) suggest that any remaining unhappiness can be addressed within a landlord's own *"complaints and/or arbitration procedures."*

There are further suggestions for both council and housing association tenants in paragraph 4.2 (b) and (c), by use of the Right to Repair Scheme or using the Housing Ombudsman's Service.

But I am going to put this in bold, so that it becomes fundamental to your thinking:

A social landlord is entitled to suggest that the tenant uses its own complaints procedure

So in cases involving both social housing and private tenants, landlords can suggest to the tenant's solicitors that ADR through a cost free and speedy process is attempted before the remainder of the Protocol is followed.

For obvious reasons, a local authority or housing association complaints procedure is likely to be the best means of ADR. It is free to both parties at the point of use, very speedy and potentially flexible.

How does a landlord insist on ADR after receiving an LOC?

What does this mean in practice? A landlord should reply to the tenant's solicitors, saying that it is premature to go through the Protocol, because the parties have not attempted ADR through the landlord's own internal complaints procedure.

Usually, if a landlord replies to the tenant's solicitors' LOC saying that they wish the tenant to be advised to pursue their internal complaints process, the solicitors will object. Often it is said that the tenant has already complained and it has got nowhere. Otherwise, claimant solicitors will allege that the complaints procedure is not independent and therefore can be dismissed as an option.

In my experience, in most cases, tenants have not raised any complaint at all. Even if they have, no formal complaint will have been made through the complaints process. Alternatively, such a complaint will have been made in respect of one, often small, aspect of the claim which is now being pursued. Most of the allegations made in the LOC were not included in the complaint made by the tenant.

Replying to the LOC

This therefore is the first issue to raise in a claim. The facts of every case are different and the response to the LOC must fit those facts exactly. If the tenant has taken the landlord completely by surprise, a complaint investigation should be launched into the entire claim.

If the tenant has been unhappy with dampness in the kitchen and has been asking the landlord come back to remedy it, that should be dealt with separately to those allegations which are brought to the landlord's attention for the first time in the LOC.

Of course, the likelihood is that a continuing complaint of damp in the kitchen or bathroom is the result of condensation, which might not be disrepair. But more of that later.

So the response to the LOC should be a clear statement of whether notice was given of any of the defects, and if so when, together with a reassurance in respect of all defects that they would now be thoroughly investigated under the formal complaints procedure.

Immediately upon receipt of an LOC, a check needs to be made to ascertain whether the tenant has notified you of any defects, and if so which defects and when you got notice. If there has been notice, how did you respond, when were works carried out and what was the result?

If the tenant has given you notice of defects and you have done works, has the tenant complained to you that the works were not done to their satisfaction, either within a reasonable time or to a reasonable standard?

If they have complained, was it an informal or formal complaint? You need to check your records and make sure of your ground before you reply to the LOC.

If you are going to invite a complaint by the tenant, you will need to provide a copy of your complaints procedure, or if you are a private landlord, the details of the redress scheme which enables complaints about housing conditions to be independently resolved.

In the meantime, pending the completion of that process, a landlord is entitled to argue that pursuing the remainder of the Protocol is premature. If you send a copy of the decision in *Hockett v Bristol CC*, which you can obtain from me pending its further publication, this should be enough. Otherwise I hope the above enables you to argue the point yourself.

The tenant solicitors' reaction to the reply

Such a response will invariably be extremely unpopular with tenant solicitors. There is no need for lawyers to be involved in an internal complaints procedure on either side. If the tenant is able to voice their concerns, either on the phone, by email or through a website complaints form, they can ask for repairs to be done and for compensation to be paid. In most cases this should put an end to the intimated legal claim.

But the tenant's solicitors will then make a claim for their costs. A landlord will be able to say that the tenant should not be entitled to the refund of any legal costs they have incurred.

Why should a tenant be able to pursue a complaint without lawyers?

Tenant solicitors say that their clients are disadvantaged, or unable to articulate their complaints and therefore the form of ADR is unsuitable because they are disadvantaged against a landlord. Social landlords will appreciate that this is unlikely to have any foundation. Employees are well used to dealing with people who struggle to articulate themselves.

They are acutely aware of the difficulties which their tenants can face and are sympathetic, mostly contrary to private landlords driven by profit.

It is insulting to most social landlords to be told that they will take advantage of their tenants in a complaints process. This is a point which needs to be made to tenant solicitors, backed up by evidence if necessary, in the event the claim goes to court.

The Protocol also refers tenants to a number of sources of advice and assistance about repairs rights and tenants should be referred to them by the landlord:

- Shelter's website

- the Citizens Advice website

- the Government's publication "*Landlord and tenant rights and responsibilities in the private rented sector (April 2019)*"

- the Government's guidance in social housing "*Good Practice Guidance on housing disrepair legal obligations (January 2002)*

Tenants may additionally consult, free of charge, various housing advice services depending on where they live. The result is that they need not approach the dispute without help if needed. In most cases it is not necessary to seek the assistance of someone to complain that there is a defect in a property. But if there is, there are few tenants who are ignored by social landlords and permitted to live in substandard accommodation.

All those involved in claims against social or private landlords on disrepair/housing conditions claims will need to be familiar with the content of these advice sources because: (1) they provide the guidance you will need to understand the nature of disrepair/housing conditions and to ensure your Complaints Process is up to the job of heading off claims at the pass; (2) you will need to refer tenants who are unsure about the formal complaints process to them.

Halting the use of the Protocol in the response to the LOC

As the first step in any tenant's journey through the Protocol is mandated to be ADR, landlords should stand up to threats to sue them by saying that the involvement of lawyers is premature. They should ask the tenant's solicitors to advise their client to try the complaints process.

That needs to be done by a letter which sets out the basis for the request to consider the use of ADR, and the basis for choosing the social landlord's own complaints process. The letter can be drafted using the material set out in this and the next chapter.

Chapter summary/key takeaways

- There is an obvious and pressing need for public authorities to avoid litigation if they can do so.

- Properly applied, the Protocol, its Practice Direction and Introduction together can provide the materials to steer tenants away from unnecessary claims.

In the next chapter we will look at complaints processes and the reason that they need to be overhauled by most landlords.

CHAPTER NINE

MAKING SURE YOUR COMPLAINTS PROCESS IS FIT FOR PURPOSE

There is no point in telling the court that you wish the claim to be stayed or even struck out pending compliance with your internal complaints process unless that procedure is up to the job.

Formal complaints procedures the Good Practice Guidance

All social landlords will have formal procedures in place, as they are required by the Regulator. In setting them up, they will have considered external guidance. That referred to in the Protocol is helpful and a landlord should ensure that they have followed the most up-to-date guidance. Following the White Paper (see below) this will change, but it is a good starting point.

The Good Practice Guidance is fairly brief on complaints systems. Paragraph 7 says that landlords should "*establish, maintain and publish system for dealing with complaints about administration (not about condition) and provide a safety net such as an arbitration procedure*". It says that "*adopting a clear and well-defined-posted complaint procedure may help reduce the need for legal action to be threatened by dissatisfied tenants. it may also highlight problems within the systems and procedures which will inform reviews.*"

Making sure the process is up to the job

Paragraph 7.02 says "*to provide a viable alternative to legal action and not a sop, any such scheme or procedure should be set-up in such a way that it can be seen to be independent and have enforceable sanctions. It should also be able to order works and award compensation.*"

It gives the example of a local authority which has a Housing Appeals Panel (sub-committee) to which tenants can appeal against a decision to go to court asking for an order seeking possession.

It says *"This is a 'last chance' but the panel requires information as to any disrepair and conditions before making a decision on whether to seek possession. Therefore an inspection of the property is carried out to ensure that the property is not in disrepair and, where it is, that any repairs are undertaken before the appeal is considered. There is also an arrears management system in operation that would normally pick up disrepair issues before any action for possession was threatened. This helps avoids* (sic) *any counterclaims to possession action* (sic).

Note the suggestion that the complaints procedure must not be a "sop", so that it should be set up in a way which demonstrates independence and has 'enforceable sanctions', whatever they may be.

Independence from the original repairs staff

So it is obvious that any complaints procedure which relies on the officer or employee who was supposed to be carrying out the repairs themselves is clearly susceptible to challenge. It is important to institute a procedure which avoids any such suggestion.

For instance, a team can be appointed specifically to look at complaints of disrepair. That might include at its initial stage, an investigation by a more senior surveyor or employee who are familiar with the repairs process.

They can investigate the complaint, looking at whether there has been notice of defects and, if so, what the repairs team have done in response to reports. They will need to visit the property, carry out an inspection, talk to the tenant, take photographs and extract the repairs history to study it and correlate it with what the tenant says.

They also need to be familiar with or investigate other housing in the area, as they need to form an opinion whether the standard of repair is reasonable, and falls within section 11 (3) of the 1985 Act and whether the home is reasonably fit for human habitation. We will look at this in more detail later in the book.

The 2020 White Paper

The Social Housing White Paper published on 17 November 2020 and updated on 22 January 2021 as the "Charter for Social Housing Residents" has addressed complaints and redress procedures. The Grenfell Tower enquiry found that tenants had raised concerns about the safety of the building but they had been repeatedly ignored by the landlord.

So it has become imperative to make those procedures more robust and an entire chapter has been devoted to it in the White Paper. By the time this book is published it will probably be enshrined in new regulations or formal guidance. The four commitments that the government has made are as follows:

- it will ensure that landlords self-assess against the Housing Ombudsman's Complaint Handling Code by 31 December 2020

- a communications campaign will be launched to make tenants aware how to raise complaints and give them confidence in the system. Organisations will be expected to inform tenants clearly how to make complaints

- legislation will be passed to ensure clear co-operation between the Ombudsman and the Regulator for Social Housing, so that landlord can be held to account more effectively when things go wrong

- the details of Housing Ombudsman complaint findings will be made public

As I write this, a consultation is underway to determine how the Housing Ombudsman service can become more responsive and "impactful". By the time of publication, no doubt measures will have been introduced to perfect the service. We need now to look at the Ombudsman's Complaint Handling Code.

The Housing Ombudsman's Complaint Handling Code

The Ombudsman published a code of practice in July 2020, which *"promotes the progressive use of complaints, providing a high-level framework to support effective handling and prevention alongside learning and development."* It is available at: https://www.housing-ombudsman.org.uk/wp-content/uploads/2020/11/Complaint-Handling-Code.pdf

The Code points out that:

> *"Some landlords see complaints as a form of negative feedback. In fact, there are many benefits to be gained from having an effective, efficient complaints process:*
>
> • *Complaints allow an issue to be resolved before it becomes worse. Those not resolved quickly can take significant resource and time to remedy*
>
> • *Involvement in complaint resolution develops staff decision-making and engagement*
>
> • *Complaints provide senior staff with a window into day-to-day operations allowing them to assess effectiveness*
>
> • *Good complaint handling promotes a positive landlord and resident relationship."*

The Code has some elements which are compulsory and with which member landlords must comply, but the Ombudsman understands that landlords will need to adapt their complaints policy and processes to meet the needs of their particular residents. Examples of this which spring to mind are social landlords with a high proportion of supported accommodation, or those with very large or very limited housing stock.

It is only in areas where the Ombudsman believes that there must be a clear and consistent practice by all landlords that it is obligatory. Social landlords must self-assess against the Code on a "comply and explain basis. The Ombudsman can issue "complaint handling failure orders" if it finds complaint processes wanting.

The Code can also be used by tenants to help them understand what they can and should expect from their landlord when making complaints.

I anticipate that every social landlord will have put into operation a process to address the provisions of the White Paper and I assume that there will have been substantial compliance with the Code. Landlords may have had to change their complaints policy as a result of the content of the code.

Parts of the Code bear closer examination, as they remain relevant to every housing disrepair LOC, so we will look at them here.

Exclusion of certain complaints

Some complaints processes exclude certain types of complaint from their ambit. Any exclusions have to be justified by valid reasoning. Only in cases where an exclusion is clearly set out should the policy exclude complaints. The examples given are instructive:

- 'stale' complaints, e.g. where the issue occurred over six months previously, unless it is a recurring issue in which case a landlord should consider the older issues;

- matters which have already been the subject of a complaint which has been determined

  and, most important:

- complaints where legal proceedings have been started, in which case there may be valid reason to exclude the complaints process, but *"landlords should take steps to ensure that residents are not left without a response for lengthy periods of time, for example, where a letter before action has been received or issued but no court proceedings are started or settlement agreement reached"*. This means that the complaints process should still be open to a tenant where an LOC has been received.

A decision that a complaint is not suitable for the complaints process must be communicated to a tenant in detail and must be also be amenable to challenge through a complaint to the Housing Ombudsman.

Complaints procedures must be accessible and visible

The Code requires landlords to make it easy to complain., And those with disabilities or particular needs have to be catered for by making reasonable adjustments. This can be important with social housing tenants. For instance, approximately 20% of tenants will not have access to the Internet, or to a smartphone.

Therefore it is not enough just to include information on the website on how to make a complaint. Residents need to be told in leaflets and newsletters how to make a complaint. Housing officers and customer facing employees will need to be astute to identify when to encourage a complaint.

If the complaints process does not result in a resolution of the dissatisfaction, the tenant needs to be told of their right to complain to the Ombudsman.

When a landlord is able to say with confidence that all its tenants will be aware of the complaints process, it can confidently tell the tenant's solicitors that their client either is aware of their ability to complain, or would be so if they had made the smallest effort to do so.

If a court is being asked to stay a legal claim, it is important to be able to show that the complaints process is highly visible and accessible.

Basic Requirements of a Complaints Handling Process

The Code provides basic guidance on the formation of a complaints process, and envisages that a Complaints Officer will be appointed in every organisation, although for some smaller landlords, that person may have other roles.

There are basic requirements for a Complaints officer are that they should:

- be able to act sensitively and fairly

- be trained to receive complaints and deal with distressed and upset residents

- have access to staff at all levels to facilitate quick resolution of complaints

- have the authority and autonomy to act to resolve disputes quickly and fairly

This means that they cannot be very junior members of staff, because they will not have the authority to investigate other staff members effectively, and are unlikely to have the knowledge and experience to be able to resolve complaints satisfactorily.

In disrepair cases, they will obviously also need a high level of technical knowledge, both of building surveying matters and of the repairs and maintenance policies of the landlord.

But paying the salary of a fairly senior employee to do this work is likely to save very substantial sums in legal fees which would otherwise be payable to the landlord's own legal team and, if it all goes wrong, to the tenant's solicitors.

As the Code says, a tenant is *"more likely to be satisfied with complaint handling if the person dealing with their complaint is competent, empathetic and efficient."*

Usually a Two-Stage Process

The Code stipulates that a process must be followed when a complaint is received. It mandates that complaints procedures must comprise of two stages, so that tenants can challenge decisions by correcting errors or sharing concerns in an appeal process.

Additionally, the Ombudsman encourages participation of other residents and/or senior executives outside the complaints team as part of the review process.

The Ombudsman does not believe a third stage is necessary in the complaints process, but does allow landlords to create one if they strongly believe it is needed. But landlords with a three-stage process will have to provide reasons for it as part of their self-assessment.

The Ombudsman sees its role as being a natural third stage in a complaints process.

Full records of complaints, reviews and the outcomes must be kept, along with all the correspondence and reports, surveys etc. this means that the digital systems must be fit for purpose and the results and documents created must be easily found if there is a later court case.

Complaints Process Findings

When a complaint has been investigated, either with or without the tenant's input, the landlord will need to set out the finding in writing

The Ombudsman also mandates maximum timescales for responses as follows:

- Logging and acknowledgement of complaint – 5 working days

- Stage 1 decision – 10 working days from receipt, or if not possible, within a maximum of 20 working days

- Stage 2 – 20 working days from request to escalate – if not possible within a maximum of 30 working days without good reason

- Stage 3 – (only where a landlord believes it is absolutely necessary), within 20 working days from request to escalate. Any additional time will only be justified if related to convening a panel.

Summary of requirements relating to Complaints Processes

The White Paper will make the issue of Complaints Processes come to the fore for every social landlord. This is an ideal and opportune moment to begin to discourage disrepair litigation by giving complaints processes the prominence they deserve.

The CPR, their PDs and the PAPs already provide sufficient ammunition for a landlord to argue that a claim should not proceed to litigation until the internal complaints procedure has been exhausted.

In the near future I hope that this principle will be strengthened by the government, so preventing many unnecessary disrepair claims.

Chapter summary/key takeaways

- Landlords have available to them all the necessary machinery by which to argue that a disrepair claim should not proceed until ADR has been attempted.

- It is possible to make an application to stay or even strike out claims which have been pursued in defiance of the necessity to consider properly the availability of a cost-free alternative to litigation.

In the next chapter we will consider the machinery of a landlord's formal Complaints Process and how it should work in practice.

CHAPTER TEN

THE MECHANICS OF THE COMPLAINTS PROCESS

Assuming that the complaints process is up and running, those dealing with disrepair claims have to look for specific features. After complaints are resolved the question of costs may be raised by the claimant's solicitors.

Completing the complaints process

If your process is staffed by competent people who can dispassionately and effectively investigate the history of the property, work out why any defects exist and whose fault that might be, you will be able to respond to a claim with the sort of detail and accuracy which enables a landlord to dispose of the claim.

A properly investigated complaint will have a full diagnosis of the nature and history of every defect, whether the landlord knew or should have known about it and whether the landlord's response was reasonable.

Often disrepair claims include numerous defects which in fact have never worried the tenant. That much is usually obvious from the repairs history, but it is important to hear it directly from the tenant themselves, because it determines the true ambit of the claim and will dramatically reduce the amount of work a landlord needs to do if the claim continues in court.

Visiting the tenant

Provided the tenant is cooperating in the process, care should be taken to obtain the history of their dissatisfaction directly from them, by talking to them in person if possible. That process will invariably elicit information that can have a determinative effect on the decision.

So the Surveyor who makes the inspection should be tasked with running through the list of defects with the tenant, checking when they believe they reported them and confirming whether or not the defect is in fact something they want rectified.

In my experience, most tenants will immediately make it clear which defects concern them and which have been brought to their attention only by the visit of a claims management company employee or a surveyor.

Using the information gained from the survey/visit

Such information needs to be taken into account in deciding first whether there is any merit in the complaint, in respect of each defect, and second whether any works are necessary and compensation payable.

Often tenants will frankly tell their landlord that they are not worried about certain of the works identified by their solicitors on the LOC. That information may not be known to the landlord unless the complaints process takes place. It is otherwise only reliably discoverable at trial -not ideal.

This does not have to be a complete legal analysis, although it is essential for the officer to be able to identify disrepair and unfitness. Complaints processes can deal both with disrepair allegations and with service failures, whereas the court will only be tasked with deciding whether there has been a breach of the legal duty to repair. That distinction is fundamental

Service Failures vs Disrepair/Unfitness

For instance, a tenant may be complaining about condensation dampness, which would be preventable if they were given the right advice and assistance, or if improvements or design changes are made to the property. There is normally no duty under the old law, either in contract or under section 11 of the 1985 Act.

But condensation might be so bad that a property is unfit for human habitation. Most of the time it is not an issue, although many tenant surveyors may say that the condensation is so bad that it renders the home 'unfit' under section 9A.

Under the new law there will be many cases where landlords might feel it expedient to carry out design improvements to reduce condensation rather than argue about whether the home is 'unfit' as alleged. It is obvious that this will cause a significant increase in repairs expenditure over the coming years.

The assistance might also include referral to agencies to help with debts and financial management, the provision of physical assistance at home or of furniture or floor coverings.

A complaints process should look at service failures as well as breaches of duty and there may be cases in which tenants should have received a different or better service, although there has been no breach of repairing duty. Thus recommendations for works and payment of compensation may be made within the complaints process when a tenant would not recover anything in a legal claim.

Compensation payments

If the Complaints Process is to provide a genuine alternative to litigation, a tenant ought to be able to recover within it a similar amount to that which they could expect at court. Compensation for service failures is historically very much lower than that obtainable within the legal process. There is an obvious reason for that where it concerns service failures, but if dealing with a breach of the legal duty to repair, complaints officers need to know the appropriate compensation levels. For present purposes, it is enough to mention that damages for disrepair can be calculated in various ways and practitioners will need to be familiar with the principles in a number of cases[8]. For further details see D & R and Housing Conditions.

---

[8] including *Calabar Properties Ltd v Stitcher* [1984] 1 WLR 287, *Wallace v Manchester City Council* (1998) 30 HLR 1111 and *English Churches Housing Group v Shine* [2004] EWCA Civ 434

Communication of complaints decisions

Complaints decisions should be provided in writing, in narrative form. A good complaints process will produce a decision letter which is often a number of pages long. Undue brevity may indicate a lack of proper analysis of the history of defects.

A complaint finding will give a clear outcome-either upholding or dismissing the complaint in respect of each individual defect. If there is a finding that works are necessary and have not been carried out, there will be a list of recommendations as to works, and if appropriate, an offer of compensation.

I have included in Appendix 1 an example of a response by Chief Executive to a Stage 3 complaint, in which the tenant was already unhappy with the state of repair of her property when the landlord began possession proceedings for rent arrears.

Benefit of the complaints process

Properly carried out, a complaints process should address the concerns raised by the tenant in their LOC. If it does not do so, it means either that the process is inadequate or that the tenant's solicitors are unduly optimistic.

If proceedings are then commenced, they can be defended on the grounds that the tenant has already been compensated. The complaints process does not replace litigation and decisions must not be made "in full and final settlement" of any legal claim.

They should compensate for loss of amenity and therefore will be taken into account in any subsequent claim, but they must not supplant the legal process. Thus tenants should not be asked to sign confirmation that the payment is made in full and final settlement of their claim, or any similar such wording.

Claims for costs following completion of the complaints process

If the claimant has been persuaded not to pursue their claim until they have tried the complaints process, only if it fails to satisfy the claimant should the steps in the Protocol be continued.

But claimant solicitors might still ask for their costs. If the claim has been resolved within the complaints process rather than with the assistance of lawyers, those costs are not payable.

Claims for costs following settlement under the Protocol

Of course, if acting within the protocol, landlords who carry out repairs in response to a claim will have to pay the costs if they settle in certain circumstances-on the authority of *Birmingham City Council v Avril Lee* [2008] EWCA Civ 891.

It is only when the involvement of lawyers in a claim is justifiable that a claimant can expect their reasonable costs to be met, and then only *"according to whether the claim would fall within the FastTrack or the small claims track if it were to be made in court."* (Paragraph 16).

Hughes, LJ said (at paragraph 33) that the object of the Protocol *"is very clearly that, provided the claim was justified, it ought to be settled on terms which include the payment of the tenant's reasonable costs: and costs calculated according to the track which the claim would fall to if made by way of litigation."*

Pre-allocation costs are not affected by allocation-the court's powers in respect of costs are unrestricted in relation to those costs. Therefore, an order can be made in respect of them if it is necessary *"in order to ensure that the protocol does not operate to prevent recovery of costs reasonably incurred in achieving the repair."* (paragraph 35).

Costs will be ordered on the FastTrack basis at the date on which repairs are carried out if the claimant subsequently wins at trial. Otherwise, there is no means of recovering those costs, so claimant will have to bring a claim in order to pursue them.

Obviously, if a landlord did not know of the defects alleged (as is often the case in respect of most defects) then at trial the tenant will not win. Liability might not be established at all, or only be established in respect of one defect, the repairing costs of which would be minimal. The court would be likely to say that the claim was not "justified", so the claimant would not be entitled to their costs.

Additionally, it is only when there was a well-founded claim for specific performance at the time solicitors had to follow the PAP that a defendant landlord should pay costs on the Fast Track basis. A claim for housing disrepair will be allocated to the Fast Track when the judge is of the view that there is a valid claim specific performance and either the claim for damages is worth more than £1,000 or the cost of the works necessary is over £1,000.

If the complaints process has run its course, by the time solicitors are involved, there should be no outstanding works. So if the initial approach by the claimant's solicitors has been rebuffed with a direction that the complaints process should be exhausted, by the time they are involved, there should be no reason that specific performance is necessary at all.

This should result in a decision by the court that the case was never one which would have been allocated to the Fast Track and that only Small Claims Track costs are recoverable.

TA

The quantum of costs in disrepair claims settled under the Protocol

In *Birmingham v Lee* the court made observations by way of a postscript (at paragraph 37). They were not asked to deal with costs recoverable but said that "*somethings ought to be made clear.*" Even at the stage of the allocation questionnaire, the claimant was saying that her costs were about £7,100. The court observed:

> "*We do not know whether there is some special reason for such a level of costs, but Mr Luba did not attempt to suggest that they were justified. We say no more than that, unless there is some special factor, costs at that level look prima facie vastly disproportionate, and that if costs ever fall to be assessed they will need to be scrutinised with some little care.*"

This is a warning which is ignored by many claimant solicitors. If a landlord does settle using the Protocol, they can expect often exorbitant claims for costs, of between £5,000 and £10,000 when no work has been done other than the issue of a LOC and some negotiations, perhaps the obtaining of a surveyor's report. Such costs are clearly totally disproportionate to almost every disrepair claim encountered.

Claims of that nature can be contested by the instruction of good costs lawyers. They should never be paid without challenge.

Chapter summary/Key Takeaways

- An efficient complaints process should put an end to most disrepair claims, but if it does not do so then it should at least protect against a claim for specific performance of the repairing covenant and part, if not all of the damages. That is likely to have consequences in costs.

- If a landlord has instigated its formal Complaints Process and its officers have made a proper investigation and findings, the tenant should be satisfied with the state of repair of their home and with any offer of compensation.

- Claims settled under the complaints process should not involve the payment of a tenant's costs. As the claim was resolved through the complaints process, rather than litigation, it was not "justified" as per *Birmingham City Council v Lee.*

- If the complaints process fails to placate a claimant, or more likely, their solicitors, the claim will carry on.

In the next chapter we will look at the identity of the claimant, the nature of the property and the locality, all of which are relevant to assessment of the merits of the claim, whether under the complaints process, the Protocol or the legal claim.

CHAPTER ELEVEN

THE IDENTITY OF
THE CLAIMANT

The identity and type of occupants – why is it important?

The Protocol requires that the claimant is identified. This requirement can be of fundamental significance. Occasionally the LOC provides the name of an occupant who is not even the tenant. They may mistakenly believe that they have a joint tenancy, but enquiries reveal that it is in somebody else's name. While this may not stop a claim being made, the nature of relief available changes.

Claimant solicitors are unwilling to pursue claims made by occupants rather than tenants, because ordinarily they have no contractual remedy, so such claims are usually restricted to cases where physical injury has been caused to an occupier.

The LOC rarely says who else is living at the property other than the tenant. That can give rise to a problem, because after settling one claim, a landlord may face further, additional claims from other occupants who are said to have suffered as a result of the disrepair.

Other occupants

In the main, it is the tenant who will be entitled to make claims, because they can rely on section 9A and section 11 of the 1985 Act. Other occupants can only succeed if they successfully argue that the Contracts (Rights of Third Parties) Act 1999 gives them the right to sue under the tenancy or in statute. For instance they may be named on the original tenancy as occupants and will be presumed to benefit from the terms of the statute/contract.

More commonly, other occupants in the house are provided for under the claim of the tenant, on the basis that the tenant can claim for their benefit as well as for themselves. Damages will be limited, as they are just hangers-on to the claim, but as it is only the tenant who is paying rent, there is some justification for this principle. Additionally, it is the responsibility of the tenant to provide a comfortable home for the other occupiers, so if they recover damages for themselves, those occupiers might expect a share of those damages.

There are limited circumstances in which other occupants can bring claims, but only where they have suffered injury or damage to their property. They can then sue under the Defective Premises Act 1972 or the Occupiers' Liability Act 1957 in respect of injuries incurred in the common parts. Such claims are relatively rare.

Therefore, whenever dealing with a claim, if you are going to settle it, you will need to confirm who is resident and to ensure that you get confirmation from all occupants that the settlement reached is in full and final satisfaction of all claims which could possibly be made by any occupant. If you do not obtain such confirmation, you may be in for an unpleasant surprise.

Costs in cases where additional claims are brought

If a claimant solicitor does issue a subsequent claim, they may be at risk as to costs: see the case of *Chin v Hackney LBC* [1996] 1 AER 973, CA. If there is no adequate explanation as to why the subsequent claim was not brought at the same time as the original one, the claimant's solicitor might be liable for any costs wasted by the landlord because of the duplication of work in the second set of proceedings.

The individual characteristics of the claimant

It is necessary to think carefully about the individual characteristics of the tenant concerned. There may be reasons why they are experiencing particular problems with the property. This sort of information should be on your tenancy file and will form part of disclosure in the event the claim proceeds. Otherwise, it needs to be considered within the complaints process.

Is there a 'typical' claimant?

Knowledge of the particular abilities and limitations of tenants is important in terms of the landlord's maintenance expectations. Estate management must take into account what can be expected of the person who covenants with the landlord.

A landlord will need to consider what each individual claimant tenant is capable of doing in terms of property care. Tenants may be unable to comply with the requirements of the tenancy.

In my experience, the majority of claims in which I have been instructed have been brought by female tenants, either living alone or with children. This may be because 55% of all new lettings were made to single adults, and very few to couples or couples with children (7% and 11% respectively) and in 2019–20, 23% of social housing tenants were single females and 18% were single males (English Housing Survey 2019/20). There is a great need for such accommodation – in 2018/19 21% of social housing lettings were made to a single adult with one child or more and 93% of those tenants were women. There may be reasons why they struggle with internal conditions-lack of available free time because they're working too hard, poverty, or children who cause damage.

Unexpected claims

In the past there were few claims from some tenant groups e.g., couples with children, single men, tenants of advanced years. This may be of no relevance, but when there is an unexpected claim, you might consider whether there is anything unusual or special about the tenant or a member of their family which has an impact on the physical condition of the home.

For instance, I have come across cases where children with autism or schizophrenic adult children have caused significant damage in the home. Of course, such damage must be treated sensitively when reported by a tenant. But in my experience claimant solicitors and their surveyors often include it within the allegations of disrepair. It is frequently not reported, presumably because the tenant is worried that they will be made to pay for it.

In one claim by a middle-aged man with no apparent disabilities, my clients were surprised to receive a counterclaim for disrepair on a rent arrears case. After careful investigations, we discovered that he had been living and working in London, drug-dealing. He had sub-let the property illegally and his tenants had failed to report any of the defects which arose. Over time rent arrears had accrued.

His solicitors had not been able to discover the real reason for the arrears and made the counterclaim in good faith, on legal aid. The landlord obtained evidence mostly from neighbours, but also from the police, given the fraud uncovered. The disrepair counterclaim was dismissed and a possession order made against him.

Poverty-related issues in social housing

Poverty is more of an issue in social housing than in private stock. About 77% of private renters are employed (67% in full-time work and 10% in part-time work) with 8% retired and 4% in full-time education, as against in the social housing sector 45% in employment (31% full-time, 14% part-time) and 25% retired. 47% of social renters were in the lowest income quintile, 24% in the second lowest, in stark contrast to the private sector. This has an obvious implication for fuel poverty and ability to maintain/decorate.

Disability issues in disrepair claims

In my experience disability is rarely an issue in claims. The landlord must check whether there are any health issues which will have an impact on the care of the property. Your repairs policy will consider the individual needs of tenants and should ensure that they are not left unable to care properly for their home.

Most tenancy conditions provide that the tenant will be responsible for decorations. Often part of the cause of problems is either a total lack of decoration, or infrequent/sub-standard attempts at decorative works. There is a continuum, from the tenant who moves in, does not ever even put down floor coverings and never decorates, to the tenant who is fastidious about their living conditions and decorations.

As the person dealing with their disrepair claim, you need to think about where they fall along that line and think carefully about whether your assessment has any implications for your future conduct and your approach to the case.

The impact of the occupier on the property

There are obvious implications for the tenant who either has insufficient resources or skills to look after their property properly.

An unintended result of compliance with the Decent Homes Standard has been a dramatic reduction in the fresh air circulation in social housing. Landlords have invested in the sealing of fireplaces and the blocking of other sources of draughts. UPVC double-glazed windows, cavity wall and other insulation have been installed. Draughty Crittall windows have been replaced with perfectly sealed units which have trickle vents. Those vents can be closed manually, or blocked using Sellotape etc.

Taken together, although these requirements may have improved living conditions for some, they have caused substantial condensation problems for many others. We will look at this more carefully later.

Damage caused by the tenant's acts or omissions

If they fall on hard times, many tenants struggle to pay their heating bills and. As a result, they turn the heating thermostat down and try stop warm air leaving and cold air from entering. Many tenants remove the fuse from their ventilation fans, or otherwise disable them. They close trickle vents, block air bricks/Brook vents etc.

The tenant might supplement or replace their heating by using an unvented or condensing tumble dryer, with the exhaust hose venting into the property. Alternatively, they might dry clothes on the radiators, with the windows closed. They might cook without any ventilation, either by way of opening the window or using the extractor fan. They may use propane gas heaters.

In almost every case, one or more of these factors is a substantial cause of problems with living conditions in the home. It provides the backbone

85

of many disrepair claims, when the tenant's acts and omissions become either the whole or part of the cause of defects in the property.

These issues will need to be addressed in the report which has to be prepared in response to the claim. Whether a landlord is proceeding with a formal complaint, or responding through the Protocol, an immediate visit to the property is essential, with the aim of preparation of a full report into each of the defects and the history of notice and repairs to every one of them.

Chapter Summary/Key Takeaways

- Think about who is living at the property. Make enquiries and confirm that the tenant is there full-time. Check who is living there with them.

- Make a thorough investigation of their living circumstances and consider disabilities.

- Use the information as part of the report, to consider and determine whether the living circumstances are the cause, in whole or in part, of any or all of the defects.

In the next chapter we will consider the standard of repair necessary according to the Act and how that affects liability.

CHAPTER TWELVE

THE DEFECTS ALLEGED –
DOES LIABILITY ARISE?

The subject headings of the LOC in the Protocol address the question of notice before it requires the claimant's solicitor to list the defects. This sometimes shifts the emphasis of the claim away from a central issue. It is all very well that a landlord has been told about a problem in a home, but that problem must amount to actionable disrepair if the tenant is to succeed in their claim.

Often the LOC includes defects which are not actionable. There is a great deal of law on the definition of disrepair, to which must now be added consideration of 'unfitness'. This is a practical book, about how the landlord responds in terms of processes, rather than a book of analysis of the law behind the claims, so we will look at defences first, concentrating on the likely allegations made in the LOC.

The standard of repair upon receipt of notice

In general terms, whether a defect occurs in the premises or outside, a landlord is liable in damages for loss of amenity if the tenant has given notice of the defect and fails to repair the property to an acceptable standard within a reasonable period, or it is repairable without notice.

But that rule is not absolute, e.g. it is subject to the general restrictions on the standard of repairs, to the principle that patch repairs may suffice and to other restrictions.

Defences to claims of breach of duty

Before thinking about individual examples, it is necessary to consider the circumstances in which a landlord is not liable for the loss of amenity caused by defects in the home even though they might be within the repairing covenant.

Now that unfitness is a criterion, the question whether a defect is repairable is more subtle. For instance, it is no longer true to say that defects in design do not usually give rise to a liability to repair. Subject to that distinction, there are still some principles relevant to the question whether, taken as a whole, the property can be said to be in actionable disrepair.

Claims where the defects are too small or too large

There are two broad reasons why a claim might fail because the defect is not actionable: first because, despite the presence of defects, the home is in a reasonable condition overall and second, because the property is near the end of its prospective life and the ordinary standards do not apply.

Prior to the coming into force of the 2018 Act, a defect in a property caused by design issues could not give rise to liability, so that a house which was otherwise in good structural repair but did not perform its function well (e.g. because it generated copious condensation as a function of its design) could not be said to be in disrepair. It is now necessary to look separately at the question of fitness for human habitation, so in this section we consider whether the structure and exterior is out of repair.

Limits on the standard-section 11 (3) of the 1985 Act and common-law

Everyone dealing with disrepair claims should have at the forefront of their mind the wording of section 11 (3) of the 1985 Act: "*In determining the standard of repair required by the lessor's repairing covenant, regard shall be had to the **age, character and prospective life of the dwelling-house and the locality in which it is situated**".

This subsection of the Act sets the standard to which repairs must be carried out. Homes, whether rented or owned by their occupants will rarely be in a perfect state of repair. The purpose of section 11 of the 1985 Act was not to impose an impossible standard on landlords. The key concept is reasonableness.

Put simply, to satisfy the 1985 Act a rented home subject to a tenancy of less than seven years need only be in a *reasonably* good state of repair.

That standard is to be judged by the standards of similar homes of that age in that area.

Although that word is not used, if landlords work at being reasonable, they are unlikely to be criticised by the court. Of course, the tenancy might impose a higher standard. This does not necessarily follow below. If the phrase iis something like "good and tenantable repair" the court is unlikely to conclude it means anything more than "repair"[9].

There is no significant difference between the statutory and the common law standard. The simplest way of looking at the limit on the standard of repair in section 11 is to consider whether the damage is either too inconsequential to merit repair, or so serious as to mean property is effectively at the end of its useful life.

Both in case law and under section 11 (3), the court needs to decide whether any damage is unacceptable, primarily in the context of the age, character and locality of the home and the objective expectations of the average tenant likely to rent such a property.

So the first question which needs to be investigated is whether, despite the existence of certain defects, the condition of the property is reasonable compared to others in the neighbourhood. It is necessary to consider this both as a whole and individually in respect of each of the defects alleged.

Providing evidence of the standard required

This fundamental question is often ignored in disrepair claims. Surveyors' reports rarely consider the issue. The court must determine whether the damage is unacceptable in the context of the four considerations.

In order to do that, the court needs evidence in respect of each aspect, individually and then collectively. This evidence should be given by an expert, because a degree of opinion may be involved, but a knowledgeable

---

[9] see for instance *Proudfoot v Hart* (1890) 25 QBD 42

housing officer may be able to help on some aspects, at least by giving the surveyor hearsay evidence of conditions in other homes in the area.

Put simply, the expert should ask whether the general condition of the dwelling the subject of the claim falls below the standard of other similar properties in the area.

If, despite the presence of the defects relied upon, it can be said that it does not fall out of the range of similar properties, the claim should fail because section 11 (3) provides a defence.

A skilled and knowledgeable surveyor will be able to describe these issues and state how they affect the standard of repair to be expected.

The age of the property

The court needs to consider the age as at the date of letting. In an 1890 case which is still relevant today, Lord Esher said that "*nobody could reasonably expect that a house 200 years old should be in the same condition of repair as a house lately built*"[10]. When he said that, he was considering the difference between a house built in 1690 and one built at the end of the Victorian age. This is different to considering the prospective life of the property.

It is the age as at the date of the start of the tenancy which is important. So you need to look at the effect of age on the building. If the property was built in 1890, it is likely to have undergone significant structural repair and improvement over the years.

For instance, such homes are unlikely to have cavity walls, and a tenant will not be able to demand that the walls are re-built to include them. Similarly, the walls are likely to have suffered settlement cracks over the years and there may be hairline cracks in the render and plaster. The floorboards may be uneven and may sag toward the middle of rooms.

---

[10] *Proudfoot v Hart* (1890) 25 QBD 42

These defects might be considered unacceptable in a modern home. But they can be seen as normal for a property of this age.

Character of the property

The court should consider the type of accommodation – put at its most extreme *"because the same class of repairs as would be necessary to a palace would be wholly unnecessary to a cottage"*, according to Lord Esher[11].

While this is as indelicately put as his other well-known comments in the case, it is fundamental. Social landlords have an obligation to provide the best housing they can to the greatest number of people possible. Shelter says *"the key idea of social housing is that it is more affordable than private renting and usually provides a more secure, long-term tenancy."* Social landlords are not concerned in the building of palaces, but in providing functional homes which are comfortable yet still affordable.

The court must consider the overall condition of the property as at the date the tenancy began. This can have a significant impact on the standard to be expected. There will often be a detail condition survey report available, although the court does not need detailed evidence of its condition.

In commenting on this aspect, a surveyor should separate the effect of anything done or not done by the tenant and other occupants on the differences between the condition when let and the date of the claim. Deterioration caused by wear and tear is repairable subject to considerations of age.

But that caused by deliberate acts or omissions of the occupants or other breaches of tenancy is rechargeable and a tenant should not recover compensation in respect of those defects, even if they are repairable.

The locality of the premises

Another brilliant quote from Lord Esher: *"the locality of the house must be taken into account, because the state of repair necessary for a house in*

---

[11] ibid, in *Proudfoot*

Grosvenor Square would be wholly different from the state of repair necessary for a house in Spitalfields".

What is the general standard of construction, type of building method, materials used, maintenance standard of the area? Are there local conditions, such as weather or geography which contribute to challenges?

These are usually questions to be addressed by the surveyor, but lay evidence can be used. There may be staff members living in the area or in this type of housing who can give relevant evidence on the peculiarities or special characteristics of such properties.

What is the tenure mix in the area? How many social housing units are there in the area? How does your performance in terms of providing housing measure up to other social landlords and private landlords? What sort of standards prevail in their properties?

Social landlords can use their performance markers/Key Performance Indicators for useful information as to their position in the quality ladder and other data. If this is not something that you wish to shout about, perhaps it is time to improve your position!

Either way, you will need to adduce evidence about it if you want to respond properly to the claim.

The population of the area and the likely tenant

Another quote from Lord Esher in *Proudfoot*: "*the condition of the premises must be such as would make (it) reasonably fit for occupation of a reasonably minded tenant of the class who would be likely to take it*".

If a surveyor is asked to comment on the question, they should be able to give evidence of the nature of the expectations of the average tenant. Are there particular problems for tenants generally found in the area or in your property – high levels of poverty or social problems which are prevalent and should be taken into account?

Are there any other claims in respect of that area? Who is bringing them and against whom? If there have been or are other cases, what has happened or is happening in them? If there are no claims against other landlords, why not?

Do any staff members live in the area or type of housing? Otherwise, are there any tenants who might be able to give you an unbiased overview of the repairs team's performance?

The prospective life of the dwelling

The 1985 Act included an additional consideration-the "prospective life of the dwelling house", which had not been specifically considered in the case law. In practice it is rarely likely to add anything in terms of a defence, because its applicability was limited by a 1987 case. [12]

It will only be of application in rare circumstances, e.g. where the landlord intends to demolish or reconstruct the whole property with vacant possession. Then it might be a factor in determining whether it is reasonable to carry out running repairs rather than more serious structural works[13].

PRC homes

With modern building methods and the drive towards remediation and restoration, it is unlikely there will be much social housing stock which has reached the end of its prospective life. The main exception is non-traditional and easily erected Precast Reinforced Concrete stock ("PRC").

Many of those homes were built after the Second World War when labour and materials were short. They were built between 1950s and 1980s, but critical structural problems emerged, particularly in the concrete, which degraded as a result of environmental factors.

They were never intended to have a significant lifespan. The Housing Defects Act 1984 classes them as "defective housing". Unfortunately, a significant number were sold under the Right to Buy legislation and

---

[12] *Maclean v Liverpool City Council* (1978) 20 HLR 25

[13] see the case of *Dame Margaret Hungerford Charity Trustees v Beazley* [1993] 2 EGLR 143

owners were left with long-term problems. They can be repaired and given a significant boost to their lives, but many social landlords have significantly reduced or eliminated them from their stock by redevelopment.

If the claim relates to a PRC home, there is a distinct possibility that the landlord will be engaged in a replacement scheme and will be reluctant to carry out large-scale expensive repairs.

Therefore, this will be one of those rare instances where a claim may be defended on the basis that the property has reached the end of its prospective life and is due to be demolished and reconstructed.

In such a case, the court is likely to sanction running repairs, rather than major works. This might mean that the tenant lives in less than satisfactory conditions for significant periods, but provided a landlord is reasonable about its approach, the court is likely to support it.

Running repairs in place of complete renewal

Any single defect might be capable of repair in a number of different ways. At one end of the extreme, when tiles are dislodged from a roof, a tarpaulin could be placed over the hole, stopping water ingress. But no landlord would suggest that should be more than a temporary, emergency repair. It is reasonable in the circumstances.

The question is then what works should be carried out to remedy the defect. A landlord then has a choice whether to carry out a patch repair of the roof, or completely to renew it. Additionally, in making those choices, the landlord might decide to use a less or more expensive type of roof tile, for reasons of economy or thermal efficiency.

The choice is a matter for the landlord to take, provided it is reasonable. There will come a time[14] when "*the only practicable way of performing*

---

[14] as it did in *Murray v Birmingham City Council* [1987] 2 EGLR 53

(the) covenant is to replace the roof altogether…". In that case the roof was part of the demise[15] and Slade LJ said that there was:

> "*no evidence to suggest that a piecemeal repair of the roof in 1976 right up to 1982 was not a perfectly practicable proposition. I, for my part, amd quite unable to accept the submission that, merely because there had been some half a dozen, no doubt troublesome, incidents of disrepair occurring during those six years, it necessarily followed from that the roof was incapable of repair by any way other than replacement.*"

That is a situation which frequently occurs. Less intrusive and expensive works are carried out, the defect recurs and different remedies are tried. Eventually a decision is taken to undertake wholesale, fundamental and expensive renewal of a part of the structure. The court should not criticise the landlord for such decisions, unless they can be shown to be unreasonable. To do that, the claimant needs to prove on the balance of probabilities that the landlord's surveyors were effectively negligent. This is not to say that the tenant should expect to live in sub-standard conditions, e.g. with a leaking roof. Each time water penetration occurs, appropriate repairs must be carried out. The point is that they need not immediately involve wholesale replacement of the roof structure.

This is a crucial concept and again, often ignored by tenant solicitors. Their misconception arises from the PAP. That tells both sides that the claimant should have a say in the repairs schedule. This is wrong in law, most of the time.

Tenants' solicitors attempting to dictate the choice of remedy

There are numerous provisions in the PAP which suggest that the tenant should be intimately involved in the choice of works, for example:

---

[15] in a case where the roof is outside the demise the landlord will be liable to repair as soon as there is disrepair, though the court may be disinclined to award damages to a tenant who has failed to report the defect or to suffer any loss of amenity as a result of water penetration before the defect is remedied.

- In paragraph 6.3 (d) "a full schedule of intended works, including anticipated start and completion dates" is to be included in the Letter of Response.

- In paragraph 7.1 (d) it says that "the expert should be asked to provide a schedule of works, an estimate of the costs of those works, and to list any urgent works."

- In the LOC provision for expert evidence says[16] "If agreement is not reached about the carrying out of works within 20 days of this letter, we propose that the parties agree to jointly instruct a single joint expert…"

So it is not surprising that since the Protocol came into force, tenants' solicitors have gained the impression that they should be involved in the decision as to which works should be carried out. This is something which should be resisted.

The choice of remedy is for the landlord

Provided the landlord is reasonable, the tenant has no legal right to dictate what should be done. If the landlord gets it wrong and fails to remedy the defect, damages may continue to accrue. But that is a risk which the landlord takes.

There are examples where a tenant might suggest works which are far more expensive than the remedy chosen by the landlord and in which the court has supported the tenant.[17] In that case, there was extensive rising damp, but the landlord refused to inject a damp proof course ("DPC"), wanting instead to carry out patch repairs to the perished plaster. The block was a relatively modern construction and had an ineffective slate

---

[16] the current version of the protocol at: https://www.justice.gov.uk/courts/procedure-rules/civil/protocol/prot_hou#8.1 duplicates provision for expert evidence

[17] see, e.g., *Elmcroft Developments Ltd v Tankersley-Sawyer* [1984] 1 EGLR 47, (1984) 270 EG 140

DPC, which had been bridged because it had been inserted below ground level and the internal walls were damp up to a height of 1–1.5 m.

The court ordered the landlord to insert an effective DPC , saying that it did not give the tenant a different thing from that which was let to them.

Defects which are too small

Repairing covenants do not require the rectification of all defects however small. So hairline cracks in plaster, a cracked pane of glass, minor defects in finishes, uneven but safe floors, nails in walls etc are not repairable. But for instance if the floor is so uneven that furniture wobbles and floorboards rise and prevent other normal uses of the room, the landlord must repair the defect.

In Elmcroft, on the issue of the standard of repair, Lord Ackner said "*To my mind it is unarguable that the state of that flat in particular, bearing in mind the age, character and locality of the flat was such as to be quite unfit for the occupation of a reasonably minded tenant of a class who would be likely to take it — very probably unfit for any tenant….*'

Despite this sensible and realistic restriction on the standard, a tenant surveyor's report will often include every last defect in the property. It follows that a landlord's surveyor will need to go through the list and consider which of them are defects that would not normally be repaired, even though they fall within the repairing covenant.

It is a question of good estate management. Some deterioration will be acceptable, particularly if remedial works would be expensive compared to the gain in amenity experienced by the tenant. If the defect is first identified and then an analysis made of whether it is causing loss of amenity, a reasonable decision can be taken as to whether to repair.

If there are defects in the structure which do not cause any loss of amenity, it might be good estate management not to expend valuable resources repairing those defects until there is actual damage to the tenant's amenity. Many decisions of that nature are matters of opinion and the court should be asked to consider whether the landlord is being reasonable.

Bringing together the four factors

It follows from the above that just because a dwelling is not in a perfect state of repair, it does not mean that it is in 'disrepair' sufficient to give rise to liability. If the damage is modest and no worse than that put up with by other reasonably minded tenants, the court will not hold the landlord liable.

Again, the landlord can rely on Lord Esher in *Proudfoot v Hart:* the home *"need not be put into the same condition as when the tenant took it; it need not be put in perfect repair."*

When damage is too serious

At the other end of the scale, if works necessary to remedy a problem are so extensive that they cannot be described as repairs, unless the tenancy provides for renewal the landlord may not be liable.

The general rule is that if the tenant is to be handed back something which is wholly different to that which they were demised, the works will not be repairs[18]. Since the coming into force of the 2018 Act, it is unwise to speculate how this principle might operate, because the remedial works necessary to remedy unfitness might involve significant improvement to the structure of the property.

When dealing with rising damp it is tempting to say that the installation of a DPC would amount to an improvement and therefore it is outside the repairing covenant. This may be true, but these days DPCs are not expensive to install and it is an argument that might not be worth making.

The more pertinent question is perhaps whether there is 'rising' damp, or whether it has another cause, e.g., condensation or salting from plaster previously damaged by flood.

_____

[18] see the judgement of Forbes J in *Ravenseft Properties Ltd V Davstone (Holdings) Ltd [1980] QB 12*

Possession claims where a home is in serious disrepair

The landlord may be able to obtain possession against a tenant living in a property which is due to be demolished or reconstructed. For housing associations this can be done under the mandatory Ground 6 (intention to demolish or reconstruct, or to carry out substantial works) or the discretionary Ground 9 (suitable alternative accommodation). For local authorities, Ground 10 provides a discretionary ground of possession where demolition, reconstruction or rebuilding works are contemplated.

In practice, when using Ground 6 or 10, although there is no requirement to provide suitable alternative accommodation, I have never come across a case in which a landlord has not done so. Tenants sometimes deny that the accommodation is suitable, for various reasons. Those arguments are outside the scope of this book.

In reality, in most cases, the question whether works are so major that they fall outside the scope of the landlord's repairing covenant is unlikely to arise. It is more likely to be pertinent where a tenant in commercial premises has a full repairing covenant.

Relevance to fitness for human habitation

There is a clear interrelationship between this question and the issue of whether a property is "reasonably" fit for human habitation. Expectations may vary according to the geographic region and the specific area. What is acceptable and reasonable for a tenant in one area may not be so in another.

Care should be taken to adduce the evidence relevant to this question as a precursor to the discussion of individual defects. Having considered both, a conclusion must be drawn whether the standard of the accommodation falls below that which is "reasonably" to be expected. In some areas, it may be considered acceptable to live with certain defects which in other areas tenants would expect to have remedied.

But it is not merely the presence of one or more Category 1 defect which will render a property 'not reasonably fit for human habitation' and the test of unfitness is not the same as the test under section 11 (3). A property might have numerous defects which would be classed as

99

'disrepair' under section 11 and would fall below the standard expected by section 11 (3) yet still not be unfit for human habitation.

A surveyor working for a landlord should be asked to provide sufficient evidence on this question to allow the court to make the judgement required by section 11 (3) and fitness. These days it will be necessary in some cases to address the issue of whether in that particular area there are any unique characteristics which affect the question of fitness for human habitation.

Should decorations be included in the landlord's repair works?

This is a point which can give rise to argument in claims. In a 1984 case[19] the Court of Appeal said that the cost of redecoration after works is recoverable. But in that case the court assumed that the house was properly decorated when the repair works were started. Equally there is no discussion in that case as to the standard of decorations expected of the landlord.

The Court of Appeal based the decision on betterment on an old case not involving landlord and tenant law decided as long ago as 1970.[20] The court in that case held that if the claimant cannot make good their loss without betterment, the defendant is not entitled to make a deduction to take it into account.

There was no discussion of the situation often encountered in social housing, where the tenant is responsible under the terms of the tenancy for decorations and, in breach of the covenant, has allowed them to deteriorate over many years, so that when repair works are done, the internal surfaces are not in any true sense 'decorated'. It would seem unjust in those circumstances that the landlord carrying out necessary repairs should be required to decorate an area which was previously effectively undecorated.

---

[19] *McGreal v Wake* (1984) 13 HLR 107, 269 EG 1254

[20] *Harbutt's "Plasticine" Ltd v Wayne Tank and Pump Co Ltd* [1970] 1 QB 447 at pp 468, 473 and 476,

There is yet to be a decision on the point involving a social housing tenancy in which there is an express clause requiring the tenant to maintain their own decorations.

However there is good reason why the rule should not apply where the tenant is obliged to do their own decorations. Although the landlord is obliged to repair the structure of the property beneath those decorations, they have no control over the decorative works actually carried out by the tenant.

A landlord cannot dictate the quality and nature of any decorations. A tenant may, for instance, choose to apply expensive wallpaper in place of a couple of coats of emulsion. I would suggest that a landlord then carrying out essential repairs for the benefit of the tenant should not be expected to redecorate using the same expensive wallpaper. Such eventualities should be catered for by household insurance.

Additionally, if there is an express term in the tenancy that the tenant is responsible for decorations, one could say that when the tenant took the tenancy they knew that they would have to remedy any damage themselves because their contractual obligation was clear. If then decorations are damaged during repairs, contractually the tenant has agreed to be responsible for reinstating them.

The solution to the conundrum might be found in another 1985 case[21] in which the court said: "*the tenant, who has very torn, damaged wallpaper which is further damaged, may well not be in a position to complain that the landlord has failed to make good consequential damage to the decorations if he is presented with an emulsion-painted wall. It may even be that the existing wallpaper is so damaged anyway that there was no consequential damage to the decorations, looking at the matter in the round.*"

The 'decorations allowance' in social housing

In practice, in social housing, it is an almost invariable practice that landlords do not redecorate themselves but provide a "decorations

---

[21] *Bradley v Chorley Borough Council* [1985] EG 801

allowance" to the tenant following repairs. That policy is always subject to exceptions, particularly where tenants are elderly or disabled, or otherwise unable to carry out decorations themselves. This seems to work satisfactorily, except when claims come to court and lawyers argue that the tenants should be entitled to the cost of getting decorators in to do the work. That meets with mixed results.

It is suggested that there is an issue of reasonableness to be considered. The rent charged by social landlords is very much less than a commercial rent. Where the landlord is carrying out repairs for the benefit of the tenant, if the tenancy requires the tenant to do their own decorations, then offering a decorations allowance in place of contractual decorating services is a reasonable custom and practice.

Such an allowance saves all tenants from the substantial increase in repair costs across the estate which would be caused if social landlords employed contractors to carry out all post-works decorations. It allows the landlord to direct its finances towards more important works. The decorations allowance point has not been considered at appellate level and there is no authority for my proposition, other than experience in front of district judges.

In a suitable case, the court can imply a term into a contract for commercial efficacy. It is suggested that the decorations allowance is a good example of the sort of situation in which the court should find that the commonly adopted practice is a reasonable compromise between landlord and tenant.

Chapter Summary/Key Takeaways

- There are fundamental, general considerations which fix the standard of repair necessary in contract and under statute.

- The court is not interested in an objective, fixed "one size fits all" standard. It is about providing accommodation which is of reasonable quality for the area. This question should be at the forefront of your considerations and response to the claim.

- Surveyors acting for landlords should provide factual evidence of the four issues raised in section 11 (3) so that the judge can make an assessment whether, despite the defects relied upon, the property is still in a reasonable state of repair. The ultimate answer to the question whether the state of repair is reasonable is for the judge.

- All this information is relevant and determinative in fixing the standard required. It will also have a bearing when it comes to fitness for human habitation, because it is part of the question whether the accommodation is *reasonably* fit for habitation.

- By providing factual material and opinions to guide and inform the assessment, an expert can give them assistance which is likely to be appreciated. Without that evidence they are unlikely to be able to form an opinion themselves, unless they happen to live in the area, in accommodation of a similar nature.

- We have looked at the fundamental limits on the standard to be expected.

In the next chapter we will look at the defects, commonly relied upon and at the sort of issues which arise in formulating a response.

CHAPTER THIRTEEN

THE DEFECTS ALLEGED

Because this is a book about responding to claims, we will look at what constitutes disrepair from the point of view of the example LOC, addressing the most common forms of allegations.

Before considering the list itself, I should point out one of the most fundamental issues with disrepair claim allegations: "damp", the 'defect' most frequently alleged, is not a defect at all. It is a symptom, or the effect of numerous possible causes. This gives rise to immense confusion in disrepair claims and often makes cases needlessly complicated.

Because dampness forms the basis of most claims and gives rise to the most serious consequences for occupiers, the relevant principles will be of application in almost every other allegation.

The defects alleged in the LOC

The allegations in the LOC are often something like:

- the property is damp throughout

- there is rising damp

- the kitchen/bathroom/living room/bedrooms is/are damp

- the cavity wall insulation is defective

- the UPVC windows are draughty and defective and the seals need replacement

- the window opening mechanisms are broken

- the windowpanes are cracked

- the toilet leaks/pipes leak

- the kitchen/bathroom ventilation fan is not functioning

- the roof and gutters are defective

- the exterior brickwork is defective

- the property is unfit for human habitation

Investigating Liability

The claimant's solicitors should have to prove in respect of each defect individually that it is repairable by the landlord. In almost every case this is either because the landlord is contractually obliged, or because statute implies an obligation. Liability can arise in common law, but that will rarely add anything to the contractual/statutory claim. Equally, claims can be brought in nuisance, but there are limited circumstances in which it will be relevant.

The source of the rights in respect of each defect is critical. Tenant solicitors will invariably write their LOC (and later the Particulars of Claim) relying on every possible legal right, without specifying in respect of each defect which of them will be relied upon trial.

This makes it much more difficult to respond to the claim, because you do not know the extent of the obligation relied upon and the way it is put. Of course, you can ask for clarification, but there are few tenant solicitors who have the inclination or ability to provide it.

So rather than approaching this book by setting out all the different rights and leaving the reader to work out which might apply in any case, we will look at the allegations and consider which rights might be relevant. The most frequent and serious of all allegations is that which normally appears at the top of the LOC – "damp throughout".

A study of the principles behind liability in cases where the tenant is suffering from "damp" will be helpful in considering many of the other defects commonly alleged.

"Damp throughout"

Usually, the list of defects includes an all-encompassing allegation that the property is damp throughout. This is rarely true. Further, even if there is damp in every room, it is unlikely to have a single cause, unless it is condensation dampness. Since 2003 the percentage of homes with damp problems has fallen from 10.6% to 3.4% as a whole.

Many properties will have some limited amount of damp of some sort, but there in social housing there are few in which damp can truly be said to be affecting the entire home.

Prior to the 2018 Act, it was often said that condensation was not actionable in County Court proceedings. That was and still is mostly true, unless it makes the home unfit for human habitation.

But just because a home is damp, it does not mean that the tenant has a good claim against their landlord. It is necessary to look at the causes of dampness to understand when there may be significant issues and when this allegation is unwarranted. A claim in which the surveyor fails to pinpoint the cause of dampness is likely to fail.[22]

Causes of dampness

Damp may be caused by water penetration from outside the home or may be caused or generated within it.

Penetrating damp caused by structural deterioration or construction

A roof or an external wall or other feature may deteriorate and allow water penetration.

If the tenant can establish that there is a missing roof tile, damage to the chimney stack or other structural defect which is allowing water penetration, the landlord will be clearly liable to repair it under the contract or the section 11 implied covenant. It is unnecessary to look any

---

[22] see for instance *Southwark LBC v McIntosh* [2002] 1 EGLR 25 and *Ball v Plymouth CC* [2004] EWHC 134

further than those sources of liability, at least in respect of damage suffered by the tenant themselves.

If damp makes the home unfit for human habitation, it is also actionable under section 9A, which we will look at separately.

Alternatively, damp may remain in the structure from construction and the landlord may be liable. In a newly built house, such dampness might be obvious upon inspection, e.g., if the walls have high levels of moisture remaining in the render when plastered.

Damp where the landlord is not at fault or responsible

But a landlord is not liable for all penetrating damp. If for instance there is a flood from an upstairs flat, caused by a neighbour leaving a bath tap running, the landlord will have to repair damage to the structure and exterior, but will not be liable for any loss of amenity, or for damage to property or to decorations caused.

Tenants should be insured against such problems, although in social housing they often are not covered. On the other hand, if the flood is caused by faulty pipework, the landlord or owner of the neighbouring flat will be liable for damage caused to others.

Damage arising from defects outside the landlord's possession or control

Equally, the guttering or roof of a building in which a flat is located may fail and the landlord of the flat affected by the damp may not have any right to access and repair the problem because they do not have any proprietary rights.

The landlord will generally have a claim under the terms of their lease from the freeholder or in nuisance against the neighbouring owner or it may be possible to enforce 'mutual' covenants in the lease to gain access.

Alternatively, maybe the freeholder cannot obtain access because another leaseholder is refusing entry. It may be necessary for the landlord to seek an injunction to force a freeholder or neighbouring owner to repair.

In such circumstances the statute protects the landlord provided he uses all reasonable endeavours to obtain, but is unable to obtain such rights as would be adequate to enable him to carry out the works or repairs[23].

Penetrating damp without a structural defect

Under section 11 of the 1985 Act, a landlord is not usually liable for the presence of damp itself which is not caused by a structural defect. Such damp can affect the property without damaging the structure. It can originate outside the property and flow into it. Usually that occurs from or near ground level and is often called 'rising' damp.

The Collins dictionary defines rising damp as *"capillary movement of moisture from the ground into the walls of buildings. It results in structural damage up to a level of three feet."* Some surveyors question its existence, but it is probably more accurate to query the frequency of its occurrence, because some types of damp can be misidentified as 'rising'.

It is rare for a property to be sitting on ground which is so damp that the structure soaks it up like a sponge. There are circumstances in which this might happen, such as a property with hygroscopic walls and no damp proof course ("DPC") which is situated very close to the level of the water table, or on a slope down which water is moving under the surface of the soil.

But such damp may give rise to liability because it renders the home unfit for human habitation.

Design vs structural defects

If there is no DPC, it is unlikely that the damp has penetrated the external wall because of structural deterioration. It is in the nature of the construction of the building. It only becomes disrepair where either the damp itself causes damage to the structure (and particularly to the render and decorative plaster), or where it can be said that the only reasonable

---

[23] section 11 (3A) added by the Housing Act 1988 section 116

way of repairing a defect is the installation of protection against rising damp[24].

The question can be phrased in terms of whether the works would involve giving the tenant back something different from the property which was demised. That would amount to an improvement, although sometimes repairs might even involve works which improve the property.

There are cases in which rising damp can be shown to have been caused by defective external works. Where the external ground level is above the DPC moisture will be able to bypass it and flow into the property.

This may have happened because the landlord has changed the ground level, for instance by installing a footpath too high, or the tenant has built up a flowerbed against the exterior wall. The surveyor will have to ascertain the root cause and thus apportion responsibility.

Equally, if somebody else is responsible for the penetrating damp, they can be joined into the claim as a "Part 20 Defendant". A landlord should not accept the blame for internal dampness caused by the acts or omissions of others.

Condensation

Alternatively, damp in a property can be caused by the condensation on surfaces of moisture vapour within a property. Readers of this book will be aware of the serious problems which can be caused by condensation.

First, it will give rise to mould growth, the decorations and then the plaster will become damp and deteriorate, insect infestation can occur and clothing and furniture will be damaged. Further it can have serious effects on the health of occupants.

Broadly, condensation can have two distinct causes – design and the occupants' treatment of the property. They are often interlinked. Most

_____

[24] cf *Uddin v Islington LBC* [2015] EWCA Civ 369, although in that case there was some evidence of an existing DPC, so it is not as helpful to tenants as might be thought

social landlords strive to remedy condensation dampness, because the DHP required them to do so. However, as discussed earlier, in reducing draughts and better insulating properties, many caused further condensation to occur (see below).

Defects in the design

Over the centuries, building techniques have changed. Older buildings may suffer design defects which cause intractable problems:

- The building may be single skin construction;

- there may be inadequate insulation in the walls and roof;

- the cavity wall insulation may have failed;

- windows may have been fitted before trickle vents were common;

- windows may not open at all;

- older properties might not have extractor fans in the bathroom or kitchen.

Condensation may also be caused by or related to the tenant's occupation and use of the property. Often upon inspection, landlords find that the occupants are causing condensation in a dwelling by their behaviour. They may have:

- removed the fuse from the ventilation fan;

- blocked air bricks or other events;

- closed trickle vents in UPVC windows;

- failed to open the windows;

- disturbed the insulation;

- failed to heat the property adequately.

Such condensation dampness did not and does not give rise to liability under section 11 of the 1985 Act or in most contractual claims, provided it is not caused partly or wholly by a structural defect.

The effect of the Decent Homes Programme ("the DHP")

When the programme was introduced in 1997 there were 2.2 million homes falling below the standard required. There were four main aims: freedom from Category 1 HHSRS hazards, a reasonable state of repair, modern facilities and services and a reasonable degree of thermal comfort. By 2010 over 1 million homes had been improved, but there were still issues of affordability for some social landlords in implementing fully all the measures required.

Shelter says that *"On average, social homes are more likely to meet the standard for 'decent' housing. They are better insulated, more energy efficient, and more likely to have working smoke alarms than other types of housing."*

In social housing, despite the DHP, reports of condensation dampness seem to have increased steadily over the last two decades. Although falling incomes (and therefore fuel poverty) may be partially responsible for this, there are other concerns.

The DHP has resulted in the hermetic sealing of homes – double glazing has been installed, door and window seals improved, homes insulated, fireplaces sealed and therefore draughts eliminated.

The unintended side-effect is that the natural opportunity for changes of air within a property will fall dramatically. Over the past decades, the use of moisture producing devices has increased – particularly tumble dryers and showers in place of baths. The moisture produced by human beings is trapped and has nowhere to go. It condenses on the walls.

The Decent Homes Standard was targeted for a review, as a result of recommendations in the Social Housing White Paper published on 17 November 2020. The two-part review was designed to understand the case for change to the criteria in the Standard and then how 'decency' should be defined.

For present purposes, when responding to a claim it is worth considering the interrelationship between the works done under the DHP and the subsequent rise in condensation levels. If the property concerned has begun to suffer from significant condensation issues, the Program will not have achieved its purpose.

Remedial works to address those issues may be expensive, particularly the fitting of sophisticated whole-home ventilation systems. But the individual capital cost of such works will be minimal compared to the potential legal costs of numerous disrepair claims. It often makes commercial sense to carry out works of improvement in such situations.

While such works should of course be done, it is important to separate any defects for which there is no contractual liability from improvements, because an injunction cannot be ordered and nor should damages be payable.

As this is often most of the issue where modest condensation is concerned, it will wholly or mostly defeat the claim. There is no reason that tenant should recover compensation for the carrying out of works which are not contractually necessary. Sometimes they are only needed because the tenant is not heating or ventilating as well as others might, but it is easier to do the works than to argue about it.

Contractual liability for condensation

In some cases, landlords agree in the tenancy agreement that they should be liable for defects in the condition of the property. There might be a covenant "*to keep the property in good repair and condition*", which would mean that mould and condensation should be repaired under the contract[25]even though they are caused by design defects.

Prior to the coming into force of the 2018 Act, it was usually sufficient to separate condensation damp from the other defects if there was

---

[25] see for instance *Welsh v Greenwich LBC* (2001) 33 HLR 40

evidence that it was either caused by a defect in design or the tenant had caused it themselves.

Liability for condensation under the 2018 Act-fitness for habitation

The 2018 Act has lessened the importance of such covenants, because provided the property is not reasonably fit for human habitation, many types of work which involve an improvement in design can now be ordered by the court. This obviously includes remedies for condensation dampness.

So today a tenant can rely on condensation damp if they can prove that the property is not reasonably fit for human habitation, and second that works can be done which will cure that condensation. To put it another way, provided the test for unfitness is satisfied, the landlord has to prove that the condensation is caused wholly or mainly by the tenant in order to escape liability.

This can give rise to complex arguments. A tenant has a contractual right to a home which is reasonably fit for human habitation, under section 9A of the 1985 Act. Part of the consideration whether it is unfit involves identifying whether there are present any of the 29 types of hazard named under the Housing Health and Safety Rating System, created by the Housing Act 2004, Part 1 ("HHSRS").

They include damp and mould growth and excess cold. Today there is very little, if any, social housing which does not have any form of heating at all.

But there may be some heating installations which do give rise to liability. For instance, it can be argued that a tenant in fuel poverty cannot be expected to heat their home using expensive electrical storage heaters. That might itself mean that the home is excessively cold. That cold, along with a lack of ventilation might also cause condensation. In any individual case, this will be a matter of expert evidence for a Surveyor, or preferably an environmental health expert.

If sufficiently serious, that condensation might stop the home from being "reasonably" fit for human habitation. If it is unfit, the landlord will be liable. They might be expected to improve the insulation and/or ventilation, and/or to replace the heating with some more economically viable method.

The 2018 Act has greatly increased the potential for liability. Today there might be cases in which liability arises under both section 9A and section 11, such as where the storage heaters are defective as well as expensive.

Distinguishing between penetrating damp and condensation

In cases where there is dampness but the home is still fit for human habitation, the surveyor will need to ascertain the cause of the damp found and, if there is both penetrating and condensation dampness, attempt to apportion the split between the two.

This can be a challenge. Often, condensation dampness can be so severe that it effectively masks the damage done by a modest area of penetrating damp. A landlord might miss such damp in their assessment of the defects in a property, particularly where there is serious condensation.

Tenant surveyors are alive to this issue and tend to inspect the exterior carefully, then often attribute internal dampness to any structural defect found, without separating the effect of condensation caused by the tenant.

That may or may not be justified. If they are right, there is obviously potential for a repairable defect to be overlooked. That might lead to liability being established when it ought not to be.

Since the 2018 Act came into force, this may not be a question of such fundamental importance. If condensation dampness makes a property not reasonably fit for human habitation, the question will then only be whether it is caused wholly or mainly by the tenant.

The scope for argument is greatly increased. There is, however, significant technological help available to ascertain the cause of the dampness.

Defending a condensation claim – property condition monitoring

In many Letters of Claim, the existence of condensation caused by the tenant is not separated from the list of defects relied upon. Instead, the claim will often include an allegation that there is black mould on the walls, without reference to the cause. It is necessary to ascertain whether the tenant has caused it, either wholly or in part.

If there is evidence that the tenant is wholly or mainly responsible for the creation of the condensation, liability will not arise. The collection of evidence is therefore critical.

It is possible to obtain such evidence from the tenant themselves, but in my experience few surveyors attending on behalf of landlords manage to probe sufficiently into the use of the property to provide the evidential basis for the defence.

Technology can come to the rescue. If a claim is received, consideration should be given to fitting a remote monitoring system.

This can be as basic as the installation of data logging ventilation fans in the kitchen and bathroom. But there are now monitoring systems such as "Switchee" available to landlords which both control heating systems and analyse the performance of the property and the cause of problems.

At the moment only a limited number of landlords have installed such remote monitoring systems. They will become more common as time goes on. The evidence they collect can be crucial.

Suppliers of such equipment are aware of potential privacy issues and will invariably have processes which protect tenants from intrusive surveillance.

The intention behind any remote monitoring system is to provide an early warning signal, whether of technical issues or of worsening living conditions. In theory, once such a unit is fitted, a landlord will be aware of issues without the need for any intervention from the tenant.

Therefore landlords should consider fitting such systems across any stock which is susceptible to condensation dampness.

Patch repairs vs renewal

We have already looked at this issue, but it is of such importance that it bears repetition when considering the issue of penetrating damp when remedying roof leaks. There is often a wide range of possible responses to a report of flooding. Of course, in most cases it would not be necessary to replace the entire structure and a patch repair would be sufficient. A tenant, or more often their solicitor, might believe that a report of water penetration through the roof should lead to the replacement of the roof covering.

A landlord need only show that they are responding reasonably to notice of a defect, provided the tenant does not continue to suffer any unacceptable loss of manatee.

The choice of method and materials is, within reason, for the landlord. Generally, if a landlord can show that there is a reasonable body of surveying opinion which would support their method of repair as opposed to the tenant's surveyor's method, the court should not interfere with that judgement.

Other defects

Damp is at the root of almost all claims, because very few other defects cause any significant loss of amenity. It is also the most complicated of all the defects which might exist, so it makes an ideal subject from which to extrapolate to other issues.

Below I address briefly claims in respect of cavity wall insulation, defective windows and ventilation installations.

Cavity wall insulation ("CWI") claims

This is a further booming area for claims farming solicitors. In the nine months between August 2017 and April 2018 Axa experienced a 1700% rise in CWI claims and the Insurance industry anticipates that there are potentially 3.5 million homes which might be affected by failing insulation.

The claimant surveyor attends the subject property with a thermal imaging camera and obtains a heat map. This may or may not show 'cold spots' caused by defective cavity wall insulation. But the claims are being made that insulation should be removed and replaced, often at a cost of many thousands of pounds. This is an area in which surveyors will need to become competent, or social landlords will need to call in external experts.

There are many possible scenarios. For instance, one might argue that a failure of insulation which has not become part of the structure, because it is comprised of loose polystyrene balls within the wall, does not amount to disrepair as the structure has not deteriorated. But damage to the plaster caused by damp ingress will be disrepair and often the most efficacious way of remedying it will be to replace the CWI.

Alternatively, the CWI might be comprised of expanded polystyrene foam, which could be said to have become part of the structure, as it binds to the internal surface of the walls. If it fails, or is incomplete, although it appears to be an improvement to the property which has not been completed competently, this might amount to an actionable defect.

For the purposes of a response to a claim, it is enough that you know to ask your surveyor either to give an opinion themselves, or to obtain independent expert advice on what is wrong and how to fix it.

Because it is sometimes outside the demise (in flats) there might be arguments about notice on CWI claims, as discussed above.

Defective UPVC windows

Following the DHP, most social housing now has plastic, UPVC windows. As they age, they need either maintenance or replacement. Capital programmes will often provide for renewal far more frequently than homes in private ownership. This can be a problem in blocks of flats where long leaseholders have to be consulted, as they are likely to object to what they see as unnecessary expenditure.

The alternative is to patch repair, by replacing glazing units, seals ad hoc, waiting until it is uneconomic to continue. The diversion of resources towards replacement of cladding will have delayed many replacement programmes.

Provided that the decision whether to patch or replace is taken reasonably, even if the claimant surveyor argues that they would specify replacement, the court should support the landlord's approach.

Broken/inefficient ventilation systems

In many claims, the claimant surveyor correctly states that the ventilation system is not functioning. Often that is because a tenant will have removed the fuse to stop it operating. Some tenants e.g. those in fuel poverty frequently or people who do not realise the damage they are causing prefer to keep the heat generated by cooking, bathing and even the use of an unvented tumble dryer within the property.

Sometimes ageing ventilation fans lose their efficiency. This may be because they are left to become so dirty that they do not function properly, or they are old and in need of a service. Inefficiency in an installation resulting from poor design is not relevant to the question whether it is in "proper working order", so a landlord will need to investigate the cause.

Most landlords will be introducing humidistat fans at least as they encounter issues with inefficient old ventilation. Those with sufficient funds will be well advised to invest in remote data logging ventilation systems, either on an individual, case-by-case basis or across their stock of any properties vulnerable to condensation.

A landlord will need to investigate the cause of any malfunction carefully, asking appropriate questions. In an ideal world, every home would have fitted a data logging fan or ventilation system which will tell the landlord whether it is working, how efficient it is and, if it stops functioning, the reason for its failure to ventilate.

Other allegations

The same principles of law apply to other defects. Frequently the allegation that the roof, external brickwork and gutters are defective is not supported by the surveyor's evidence.

119

Additionally, occasionally there is a more fundamental issue with the allegations, for instance external render is criticised when the property is brick-faced. The LOC is prepared from the initial inspection by the claims management company employees, together with comments from the tenants and it is often clear that not much thought is given to the allegations.

Sometimes, when defects are alleged with the drainage system, it is simply a matter of a blocked gutter or downpipe, but there will always be a significant additional item of work in the Scott Schedule.

Property unfit for human habitation

Following the coming into force of the Homes (Fitness for Human Habitation) Act 2018 from 20 March 2020 in respect of all properties affected by the provisions of the LTA 1985, this allegation is being made more frequently, often without any basis in fact.

That is not to say there are no social housing units which have serious problems. The English Housing Survey 2015–16 found that there were 244,122 social homes with a "serious and immediate risk to a person's health and safety 'Category 1' hazard under the HHSRS. Many of those might fail the Fitness test, although people will have been living in them previously for many years, coping with the defects.

On cursory inspection by the landlord, the reason for that lack of specificity in the allegation that the home is unfit is obvious – in fact although there are defects, it is clear that they are not unfit for habitation.

The central question in a case where unfitness is alleged involves a consideration of whether the property has defects which are so serious that no tenant can reasonably be expected to live in it.

Determining whether a house is fit

The court must have regard to the condition of the property in respect of a number of factors listed in section 10 (1) of the 1985 Act.

This repeats the list from the old section 8, being repair, stability, freedom from damp, internal arrangement, natural lighting, ventilation, water supply, drainage, sanitary conveniences, facilities for the preparation and cooking of food and facilities for the disposal of wastewater.

To that list, the new version of section 10 adds any prescribed hazard, as defined at section 10 (2) which is "any matter or circumstance amounting to a hazard for the time being prescribed in regulations made by the Secretary of State under section 2 of the Housing Act 2004".

Those hazards are, in one paragraph (!): damp and mould growth, asbestos and manufactured mineral fibres, biocides, carbon monoxide and fuel combustion products, lead, radiation, uncombusted fuel gas, volatile organic compounds, electrical hazards, excess cold, excess heat, crowding and space, entry by intruders, lighting (including natural), noise, domestic hygiene, pests and refuse, food safety, personal hygiene, sanitation and drainage, water supply for domestic purposes, falls associated with baths etc, falls on the level, falls associated with stairs and steps, falls between levels, fire, hot surfaces and materials, collision and entrapment, explosions, position and operability of amenities, structural collapse and falling elements.

The operating guidance for the rating system is contained in a 185-page book. It is extremely complicated to assess fitness and highly unlikely that any claimant surveyor will have carried out the necessary test. However, that does not mean that, in a plain case, the court cannot form its own view, even unassisted by expert evidence.

An assessment and finding either way in respect of the current occupiers of the property would be strong evidence for the judge.

But it is only unfit for human habitation if it is so far defective in one or more of those matters that it is not reasonably suitable for occupation in that condition. We will return to discussion of this issue when considering defences to allegations.

The list of 29 possible defects gives wide scope for potential criticism on the part of a claimant in the LOC. Often those assertions are not supported by their surveyor upon service of the claimant's report. Alternatively, a bare assertion is made that the property is unfit, but now

121

reasons are specified as to why it is so seriously defective as to be not reasonably habitable.

Historic case law on unfitness

Because the old section 8 of the 1985 Act had not applied to any lettings for many years, there is no recent case law on the meaning of the implied covenant. But the old case law will still be relevant to some extent. The new law has an important extension – the whole building in which the dwelling is situated is now relevant for the purposes of section 9A.

There was case law limiting the effect of the old section 8, by allowing a landlord to argue that the premises could not be made fit for human habitation at reasonable expense.[26] That is an uncertain precedent on which to rely, because the tenant conceded the point in arguing the case despite there being no statutory restriction on the expense necessary. It is likely to be challenged if relied upon, because there is no exception in section 9 (2) or (3) providing a defence of 'unreasonable expense' – see below.

Potential for unmeritorious/exaggerated claims

It is easy to appreciate the seriousness of the potential threat to social landlords from unscrupulous claimant solicitors and surveyors. If every design issue in a 200-year-old home is analysed against the list of 29 hazards, numerous problems will be identified, many of which are insoluble at reasonable expense.

For instance, single glazed windows do not provide good heat insulation and allow draughts, so create a hazard of excess cold. They might be small and limited in number, so giving rise to a lack of natural light. Stairs in such property might be steep, causing a risk of falls associated with stairs. The structure of the building may contain lead. There may be limited

---

[26] cf *Morgan v Liverpool Corporation* [1927] 2 kb 131, CA, later approved in another case

bathroom space, perhaps only providing a bathroom with WC on one floor.

But landlords are not obliged to carry out works to remedy all issues found as there are statutory defences.

Statutory defences to allegations

There are various defences to the duty to let and keep the home fit for human habitation, found in section 9A (2) and (3) which are worth setting out in full:

(2) The implied covenant is not to be taken as requiring the lessor—

(a) to carry out works or repairs for which the lessee is liable by virtue of—

(i) the duty of the lessee to use the premises in a tenant-like manner, or

(ii)an express covenant of the lessee of substantially the same effect as that duty;

(b) to rebuild or reinstate the dwelling in the case of destruction or damage by fire, storm, flood or other inevitable accident;

(c) to keep in repair or maintain anything which the lessee is entitled to remove from the dwelling;

(d) to carry out works or repairs which, if carried out, would put the lessor in breach of any obligation imposed by any enactment (whenever passed or made);

(e) to carry out works or repairs requiring the consent of a superior landlord or other third party in circumstances where consent has not been obtained following reasonable endeavours to obtain it.

(3) The implied covenant is also not to be taken as imposing on the lessor any liability in respect of the dwelling being unfit for human habitation if the unfitness is wholly or mainly[27] attributable to—

(a) the lessee's own breach of covenant, or

(b) disrepair which the lessor is not obliged to make good because of an exclusion or modification under section 12 (power of county court to authorise exclusions or modifications in leases in respect of repairing obligations under section 11).

Applying the defences-section 9 (2)

Looking at that list in section 9 (2), it is apparent that there may be a number of reasons why works would not be appropriate.

Using the premises in a tenant -like manner-section 9 (2) (a)

First, much damage is caused by tenants failing to use the premises in a tenant-like manner. Condensation dampness is at the forefront of this consideration. Black mould in any significant quantity can easily render a property unfit for human habitation.

Tenants who keep the windows tight shut, close the trickle vents, take out the fuse of the ventilation fan etc., as discussed above, cause substantial condensation problems themselves.

Most claimant surveyors will not mention that their client appears to be causing most of the condensation seen, or they may attribute signs of damp to causes other than condensation. Alternatively they might instead concentrate on features of the home which could be changed to reduce condensation.

Although these defects might be capable of rectification, at least in part, by the installation of expensive whole-home positive ventilation systems with remote data logging, there may be no need if the landlord can show

---

[27] note this does not exclude defects which are only **partly** caused by the tenant from giving rise to liability

that the tenant themselves as responsible for the condensation. If it can be reduced to an acceptable level by amendments to the lifestyle of the tenant, the landlord will not have to carry out the works suggested by the claimant's surveyor.

The essential point is that, while not all condensation might be caused by the tenant and their family, once their acts or omissions are taken into account the home will not be unfit. Evidence on this point must be adduced by comparison with other, similar properties which are not unfit.

Works necessary to rebuild or reinstate after damage by fire, storm, flood or inevitable accident-section 9 (2) (b)

This applies, e.g. to works necessary where there has been a flood from the property above.

Works to fix anything which is not part of the structure and exterior – section 9 (2) (c)

It is not likely that this section will be used often, because the tenant surveyors rarely point out issues with, e.g., the tenant's appliances.

Works which would be illegal-section 9 (2) (d)

A landlord is not obliged to carry out works which would put him in breach of any legislation.

So for instance, in a listed building in a Conservation Area, a landlord will not be obliged to install heat efficient UPVC windows in place of Georgian single glazed units. Nor will they have to tear out an old, steep wooden staircase and replace it with a modern set of shallow stairs with wide treads.

Works needing the consent of a superior landlord or other third-party-section 9 (2) (e)

This defence is only available when the landlord has used reasonable endeavours to attempt to obtain consent but has not been able to obtain it. There is much room for argument in terms of timing here-for instance, should a landlord apply for an injunction against another party in order to be able to show that he has tried hard enough.

It is likely to be of particular application in cases where there is a serious, persistent flooding problem arising in a flat above the subject property, particularly where it is in separate ownership.

Consideration of section 9 (3) (a)

This extends the section 9 (2) defence requiring a lessee to use the property in a tenant-like manner, by making it clear that the Act does not impose on the landlord any liability if the unfitness is caused by a breach of covenant on behalf of the tenant.

So covenants beyond that requiring the tenant to be "tenant-like" may protect the landlord, e.g. where the tenant is obliged to provide floor coverings to the property but has allowed them to deteriorate so seriously that the property is unfit because of trip hazards.

Section 9 (3) (a) – modifications to leases under section 12

Although it is early days, it seems there is good reason to ask for exclusions or modifications in respect of the repairing obligations in some social housing leases, given the particular structural characteristics of many properties.

The justification for an application has to arise from the benefit to tenants in general from creating exceptions to the enforcement of the new law. Landlords and tenants must apply for such exclusion or modification by agreement, so it may be that the section is of relevance where properties would otherwise be taken out of the landlord's housing stock, so that tenants can occupy attractive but less than perfect housing.

This might be particularly useful if the landlord is intending to demolish and reconstruct the whole or part of an estate but certain individuals ask to be allowed to use the accommodation on a short-term basis pending demolition.

Chapter summary/key takeaways

- A thorough understanding of what constitutes disrepair/unfitness and what falls short is crucial.

- I have attempted to provide a short guide to some of the most important issues raised in disrepair claims.

- It is not possible in a short introduction to disrepair law to provide sufficient material on which a claim can be defended. Instead, you will need to refer to the more complete works which I use and recommend.

In the next chapter we will look at how to deal with a claimant's solicitors' insistence on disclosure.

CHAPTER FOURTEEN

DISCLOSURE IN THE PRE-ACTION PROTOCOL

Disclosure is likely to be one of the first battlegrounds for landlords who upon receipt of an LOC assert that the tenant's instruction of lawyers is premature.

This is because paragraph 5.3 of the PAP requires a landlord who is responding to an LOC to provide disclosure of the documents set out in the Protocol and a landlord should refuse if such a request is made before ADR has been attempted.

That refusal is likely to provoke an application for Pre-Action Disclosure from the claimant's solicitors. Therefore you need to know how to respond.

The expense of providing disclosure

It is important to avoid having to provide disclosure unless it is unavoidable. The process of searching out and obtaining all the documents listed in the Protocol will be lengthy and expensive if it involves lawyers.

The extent of disclosure required by the Protocol

The documents which the PAP says a landlord should disclose are likely to be extensive-they include some which are easy to obtain, but some which can be difficult to access. It follows that if disclosure is unnecessary, the landlord should not agree to provide it.

- A tenant should have a copy of the tenancy agreement, including the tenancy conditions (and Handbook), but tenant solicitors always ask for the document again, without thinking to check with their client whether they need a further copy.

- The tenancy file may contain documents which should not be disclosed for various reasons and it may be necessary to redact certain documents to remove third-party names or details. However, a tenant is usually entitled to inspect the whole of their file.

- Documents relating to the giving of notice, including copies of "any notes of meetings and oral discussions" may have to be searched for in the repairs records and can be difficult to find.

- Inspection reports or documents relating to works required cannot be provided until they are created.

- The requirement to disclose "any computerised records" means in theory that a search has to be made for every document which mentions the state of repair of the subject property.

The complaints process as an alternative to disclosure

Disclosure is unnecessary if the landlord is operating their internal Complaints Process, because a tenant does not need to have access to all the documents in order for their complaint to be considered.

It is in the landlord's interests to operate the complaints process fairly and to ensure that a careful, objective investigation is undertaken. It follows that there need be no adversarial process, as the landlord should approach the complaint fair-mindedly.

Landlords operating the complaints process

If the landlord is responding to the LOC by saying that it has not had prior notice of the defects and/or that it is going to put into operation paragraph 4 of the Protocol, both stances mean that it is premature and unnecessary to engage in disclosure before ADR is exhausted.

Availability of a Data Subject Access Request

Further, the tenant has the right to obtain those documents using a Data Subject Access Request ("DSAR" or "SAR"), so the landlord does not have to instruct its lawyers to make the enquiries and obtain those documents. This can be done by the individuals in the organisation who are responsible for responding to such requests.

Those individuals are unlikely to be working at the same salary as lawyers who would be doing the same work. As a result, the exercise can be completed for a fraction of the cost. Additionally, social landlord lawyers will often be very pressed for time and any reduction in their workload is a significant benefit to the department.

Response to the tenant's solicitors' request for disclosure

For this reason, it is necessary to tell the claimant's solicitors that disclosure will not be provided, because the material is available for free by other means and because their involvement is unnecessary until ADR through the complaints process is exhausted. They should be directed to the process for making a subject access request and informed that no further correspondence will be entered into on the subject because it is a waste of the landlord's resources.

Pre-Action Disclosure applications

The tenant's solicitors may respond with a warning that an application for "Pre-Action Disclosure" will be made if the landlord does not comply with paragraph 5.3 of the Protocol. Usually, once the tenant's solicitors issue such an application, the landlord will instruct lawyers to represent it.

The test for the grant of a PAD

A PAD application is made under CPR 31.16, which is entitled "Disclosure before proceedings start". An applicant for such an order will need to adduce evidence and satisfy the court that it should make an order. The remedy is an exceptional one and the words of the rule make it plain that there are only limited circumstances in which an order for PAD should be made. The conditions which must be satisfied are set out in CPR 31.16 (3).

The threshold requirements under CPR 31.16

There are three threshold requirements and the applicant must then prove that disclosure is desirable in order to achieve one of three aims.

The threshold requirements are that:

- the respondent is likely to be a party to subsequent proceedings;

- the applicant is also likely to be a party to those proceedings;

- if proceedings had started, the respondent's duty by way of standard disclosure would extend to the documents or classes of documents of which the applicant seeks disclosure.

The discretionary hurdle under CPR 31.16

The discretion can then only be exercised if the applicant can show that it is desirable to order disclosure to:

- dispose of the anticipated proceedings fairly

- assist the dispute to be resolved without proceedings or

- save costs

Responding to a PAD application

Such applications can be defended, both on the basis that (1) there is a cost-free and swift process to obtain the personal data held by the landlord, in the form of a DSAR, and (2) because the Protocol requires the parties to consider properly whether they should engage in ADR through the use of the repairs, complaints and/or arbitration procedures.

This means that the respondent can show that it is not desirable to order disclosure to dispose of the anticipated proceedings fairly, or to save costs. Additionally, pre-action disclosure will not assist the dispute to be resolved without proceedings, because that can be achieved more cost effectively and faster using the complaints procedure.

There is much law on the subject of when the court will exercise its discretion and the argument in these applications is invariably centred on those last three elements of CPR 31.16. The relevant cases are to be found in the commentary to the White Book and the respondent lawyer will need to provide a skeleton argument setting out the landlord's case.

Now that the decision of the single judge in *Hockett v Bristol CC* is available, the argument should be easier to run.

Practicalities of the response to a PAD application

The landlord will need to reply to any PAD application received with a witness statement, setting out the factual history of the correspondence from its point of view. Often the tenant's solicitor makes an application following a formula and fails to bring to the attention of the court the landlord's reasons for refusing to provide disclosure.

The landlord's witness statement should address that fact and make any justifiable criticism of the tenant solicitors in response.

Common additional issues in PAD applications

Such PAD applications are issued in large numbers by claimant solicitors. From the way in which they are prepared and pursued; they appear to be something of a 'cash cow', as Bean LJ remarked in *Hockett*.

Applications issued in a distant court centre

Usually, these applications are issued otherwise than in the County Court hearing centre which is local to the property. Although this is permitted by the CPR, it is inconvenient and can be expensive for landlords, who have to deal with a court with which they may not be familiar. Sometimes they have to send an advocate to a court centre hundreds of miles from them. Occasionally they are issued in a court centre which is not local either to the claimant's solicitors or the landlord.

Applications asking for a PAD order without a hearing

Often the first that a landlord knows of a PAD application is when they receive an order from the court, which not only requires them to disclose numerous documents in a short space of time, but also requires them to pay the costs of the application.

This is because the applications are sometimes drafted to request an order for PAD without a hearing. Frequently, for some reason, those applications are not even served on the respondent landlord. Applications made without notice and without a hearing should be extremely rare, and are usually only appropriate in cases of urgency and where it is necessary not to alert a respondent to the forthcoming application.

Therefore, if landlords come across this tactic, they should object to the court in strong terms to the making of orders, without a hearing, but more important without notice.

Orders for costs in PAD applications

The usual order for costs in a PAD application is that the *applicant* themselves should pay those costs, even though the application has been successful. This is mandated by CPR 46.1 (2), unless the applicant can show that the respondent's defence of the application was unreasonable.

Therefore, even if the applicant in a PAD application succeeds, the starting point is that they should bear the costs themselves. They can recover them later if they succeed in a claim at trial, when they can include them in their claim for costs.

Those costs include both the cost of making the application and of complying with any order for PAD.

There is express provision for the court to make a different order, whether that is no order for costs, costs in the case or any variation on the theme. That provision, in CPR 46.1 (3) says that the court has to have regard to all the circumstances, including the extent to which it was reasonable for the respondent to oppose the application and whether the parties have complied with any PAP.

Where a respondent landlord is objecting on the basis that disclosure can be obtained free of charge and the tenant should have attempted to get satisfaction through the complaints process, these reasons should both be found to be reasonable. The tenant's solicitors' failure to comply with paragraph 4 of the Protocol is relevant to the issue of costs and the tenant should pay those costs.

This is the case even if, in the exercise of their discretion, the District Judge allows the application for the PAD, unless the landlord has behaved unreasonably.

Chapter summary/key takeaways.

- A landlord can successfully defend a PAD application.

- If tenant solicitors become aware of the pointlessness of making such applications, they may in time simply advise their clients to make an SAR rather than pursuing an application which they are likely to lose, or on which they are likely not to recover the costs.

- The single judge in the Court of Appeal has now addressed this issue in *Hockett v Bristol CC*.

In the next section of the book we will look at what happens when the tenant's solicitors issue a claim, either after attempting the complaints process and failing to gain satisfaction (which rarely happens) or when they continue to refuse to attempt ADR and instead they issue a claim.

PART IV

AFTER PROCEEDINGS ARE ISSUED

In this section we will look at the preparation of evidence and applications in the course of proceedings where it has not been possible to settle the claim without litigation.

The first task for a landlord will have been undertaken by the landlord, at least in part, when investigating the LOC and responding to it, whether by instituting the Complaints Process or by trying to agree to settle the claim.

Despite your best efforts the claim is still alive and you need to get ready to fight it in court. This involves collecting the evidence, making sure that the pleadings match the facts of the case as you now know them and ensuring that interim applications are made to deal with any pre-trial issues.

The landlord needs expert evidence to decide whether or to what extent to defend the claim. Often some of that evidence will have been collected within the formal complaints process, although the report of any surveyor involved will not be CPR 35 compliant.

CHAPTER FIFTEEN

EXPERT EVIDENCE

The opinion of a competent surveyor is fundamental to the decision whether to defend a claim, and in providing the evidence needed to do so. The expert's report needs to be CPR 35 compliant and should provide evidence on a variety of essential issues.

A surveyor will need to understand the principles behind liability – both in terms of notice and in the nature of defects which give rise to a claim as against those which a landlord does not have to repair and/or will not give rise to liability in damages.

There will be a certain amount of duplication in this chapter, in respect of the principles of disrepair law, because the surveyor needs to understand the practical application of the law content of the report

First, the expert needs to consider the condition of the property and any works necessary. This part of the report will involve a comparison with the findings of the claimant's expert. Consideration must be given to whether the works are improvements or repairs.

Additionally, the landlord's report needs to address several issues on which the claimant's surveyor is unlikely to give an opinion.

Using an employee as an expert

A surveyor in the employment of the landlord will have the advantage of knowing the system and the stock and being able to work on cases within the landlord's standard budget rather than on an hourly rate as a disbursement. This should mean that they can devote the time necessary to each job, rather than rushing a report through without proper consideration of the issues. It is also likely to be less costly.

Potential for conflict between complaints surveyor and expert

Landlords operating a complaints procedure upon receipt of a claim need to recognise the potential for a conflict-of-interest for their surveying team. If the landlord does not use an external surveyor for the expert's report, they will be fulfilling a dual role. they If the same surveyor is to perform both functions, will need to think carefully about the implications of this situation.

Ensuring objectivity in both roles

On the one hand within the complaints process it is necessary to inspect the property to recognise defects and to recommend any reasonable remedial works, while being ready to recognise breach of duty and accept blame on behalf of the landlord. At the same time, the expert appointed to deal with the claim in court has to gather the material to provide a report which can be relied on in the legal proceedings.

In fact, provided the surveyor is professional and objective, these two roles will not produce a conflict of interest for the surveyor. The duty of a surveyor compiling a report for the complaints process is to the tenant as well as to their employer-they must be fair and objective. The duty of an expert witness is not to their employer, it is to the court. This is a fundamental rule which surveyors must recognise. It means that they cannot be a 'hired gun' in either situation.

Provided they comply with that duty, their duty to their employer should be accommodated within that role as an expert to the court. It would be disturbing if the surveyor viewed their professional responsibilities as anything less than the need to provide an objectively unbiased opinion.

It might be said that there is a potential for this conflict-of-interest to arise where a landlord has a limited budget. But in my experience this does not happen. Budgets for social housing repairs tend to be significantly greater than those of many private landlords. Investment in the health of the building is seen as a priority and the economies of scale available to social landlords often result in work programmes which err on the side of generosity rather than cost-cutting.

In the report, the surveyor should address this issue head on and confirm that they recognise the possibility, so that they can honestly say that they are being objective.

Landlord surveyor's qualifications

Similar care should be taken to ensure that the expert put forward is properly qualified for the job. A landlord should ensure that the individual is objectively properly qualified

If an internal surveyor is to be used, they may not have an equivalent qualification to that of the claimant's surveyor. In the absence of equality of formal qualifications, perhaps they are more experienced and have sufficient vocational training to be able to satisfy the court that their opinion is as valid as that of the better qualified claimant's surveyor.

Claimant's expert's qualifications

Disrepair lawyers may have come across instances where claimant surveyors have exaggerated their qualifications. A check should be made with the relevant qualifying body or university in respect of any surveyor not known to the landlord.

Provision for inspection of the property

As soon as the LOC is received it is necessary to arrange an inspection whether the complaints process is going to be operated or the claim is being fought within the PAP and legal process. The PAP does provide for such visits and the tenant should have been advised not to prevent access.

The surveyor will be reporting for two reasons – to inquire whether the defects alleged exist and to diagnose their cause, and to discover from the tenant whether notice has been given for each defect and, if so, when exactly it was given. If necessary, they need to analyse the effect of any actionable defects on the tenant.

The surveyor needs to investigate the repairs records, check them against the tenant's assertions on notice and confirm or refute each.

The content of the report

A proper analysis of cause and effect is essential. A methodical approach to each defect, using the relevant scientific methods will eventually uncover the cause of each defect. In the case of dampness, that can be a challenge. Investigations can be prolonged and technically challenging, particularly where condensation is either masking penetrating damp, or greatly worsening its effects.

The surveyor will need to look separately at the history of the defects. That involves an examination of the initial allegations made in the LOC, as against what is present at the premises upon inspection.

There should then be an investigation of whether the landlord was on notice and an assessment of what has been done and whether it has been effective.

The general standard of repair of the property needs to be expressly considered, both in the context of the rent payable and of the general standard of repair of properties in the area. If a property has particular defects peculiar to its construction type, these should be explicitly discussed, in sufficient detail to allow the court to draw conclusions as to whether the standard of repair falls below that expected by section 11 (3) of the 1985 Act.

If there is any defect in respect of which there might be liability, the surveyor will need to investigate any loss of amenity and compare it with the general living conditions of the claimant tenant, as affected by their lifestyle and expectations.

The history of each defect

The repairs records will reflect the history of each defect chronologically, rather than by property area or defect type. Obviously, this is not how they appear in the LOC.

It is necessary to investigate the defects as they appear the LOC rather than as they appear in the records. This means considering multiple sources of information and amalgamating the evidence uncovered in respect of each defect to present tell the story of each. The landlord can then admit or deny liability.

The history of notice

Initially, the surveyor needs to look at the records to see whether notice has been given and, if so, when (unless liability arises without notice). If it is possible to check the incoming telephone records for instances where a tenant has called their landlord, this should be done. These records are disclosable.

Defects of which no notice has been given

There may be some allegations of which there is no prior notice. These can be disposed of, noting all of the 'no notice' allegations at the outset and dealing with them as a whole. Obviously, in respect of those defects, the landlord's response will be that investigations are to be carried out and works ordered if necessary. Those works then have to be done within a reasonable time.

It will also be necessary to check the housing file, together with the complaints records, to ensure that notice has not been given to another part of the landlord's organisation. A landlord may operate a policy requiring tenants to report defects only to the repairs team.

Provided that policy is reasonable, the court will not take issue with it. For instance, a landlord may have a policy that caretakers in blocks of flats are not required to pass on reports of disrepair. If then the tenant reports a defect to the caretaker, who informed them that it is not within their role to pass it on, the court will not find that notice has been given.

Defects of which there is evidence of prior notice

The records will usually contain one or more defects which have been reported at some time in the past. The report will need to address whether, at the date of receipt of the LOC, there was any outstanding issue known to the landlord.

It will be necessary (depending on the repairs software) to go through each individual entry and the screens behind the summary to compile a coherent narrative, showing the date of the first report (if any) and what was done in response.

Constructive knowledge

Alternatively, the surveyor should consider whether the landlord ought to have known of any remaining problems. There are two situations in which actual notice is not required – the surveyor will need to assess in respect of each defect whether liability to repair would have arisen even though the landlord did not have actual knowledge, or when there was constructive notice. Those issues have been addressed earlier in the book.

The job of the surveyor is to consider whether the tenant suffered any loss of amenity and, if so, whether the landlord could reasonably have known of any loss of amenity being suffered by the tenant, whether by the exercise of an independent obligation to inspect (e.g. contractually mandated periodic inspections) or inspections arising from a statutory duty.

This question is important because a tenant may succeed on liability even though the landlord has no idea a defect has started to affect a tenant. In those cases it will be necessary to concede liability for that defect in respect of any period throughout which a landlord ought to have or is taken to have known of the defect. It may be that, even if the landlord was aware, the defect would cause little or no loss of amenity

Contractual obligations to give notice

Most tenancies will contain a term obliging the tenant to give notice of a defect. If then a tenant fails to do so, they will be in breach of the terms of their tenancy. Depending on the wording of the clause, they may be said to have broken the chain of causation. They should not be able to claim any or any substantial damages for loss of amenity caused by defects of which they did not inform their landlord.

Failing to give notice as a failure to mitigate

Alternatively, damages will be reduced, possibly to nothing, over the period for which a tenant failed to give notice of the existence of a defect when the landlord was unaware of it, or if the landlord knew of the defect but did not know that it was causing loss of amenity to a tenant.

The surveyor will need to make a clear statement in their report in respect of any defect where it is clear that the problem existed but there is evidence that the tenant did not inform the landlord of its existence.

Tenant fails to mitigate by failing to complain

Further, if a repair does not succeed, a tenant still need to inform the landlord that the works have failed to cure the problem.

Some repairs policies provide for a post-works inspection and/or survey, to ensure that tenants who continue to suffer loss of amenity are not ignored. It is important that the landlord either obtains confirmation directly from the tenant of their satisfaction, or records that the property was left in a satisfactory condition using objective evidence (e.g. photographs and/or a written note on the file)

The effects of the defects if liability is established

But if it is clear that the landlord did know or ought to have known of a defect and they failed properly to repair it, an assessment needs to be made of the harm suffered by the tenant as a result, both in terms of duration and extent of interference with amenity.

If on investigation it is apparent that notice of a defect had been given, and works have not been carried out, or if they have been unsatisfactory, liability in damages might start to accrue.

This will involve consideration of the condition of the property apart from the defect. Often, the effects of a defect are quite obviously minor compared to the other issues with which a tenant is living voluntarily, because they have caused those conditions themselves.

For instance, in a case in which there is evidence of a problem with penetrating damp, if the majority of the damage arises from condensation which has been caused by the tenant's lifestyle, it is necessary to provide clear evidence to allow the court to draw this conclusion. Sometimes the effect of the defect will be so negligible as to make no difference to the tenant's overall enjoyment of the property.

There may be other issues-the tenant or another occupier or visitor may have caused a significant amount of physical damage themselves, or maybe failing to clean and decorate the property to such an extent that their lack of care eclipses the effects of the disrepair.

This evidence needs to be collected, both in photographic and narrative form, and included as a separate section in the report, suitably highlighted.

Confirmation whether works intended

Where a surveyor finds defects which need works, the approach should follow the landlord's normal repairs policy, preferably making it plain when works of improvement are to be offered to remedy design defects.

The surveyor will need to prepare a 'Scott Schedule' listing the defects alleged, the claimant's suggested remedy and their response, including an estimate of the cost of any works if possible. That document will be used by the court, so it is helpful to be able to add an extra column for the judge's comments if necessary.

Separating works of repair from works of improvement

Before the coming into force of the 2018 Act, there was a tolerably clear distinction between works of repair and works of improvement. Now, under the fitness provisions, works necessary to a dwelling may well include improvements to the structure and design.

This arises where there are deficiencies in the design which lead to the existence of issues making the home unfit for human habitation. Even if the home is not currently 'unfit' within the meaning of the Act, it may be good estate management to carry out such works. In the future surveyors will need to exercise their judgement carefully, balancing the findings of a claimant surveyor against what is truly reasonable and practicable.

In any case where there is an arguable assertion by the claimant surveyor that the defects in the home render it not reasonably fit for habitation, the surveyor will need to decide what in their discretion and professional opinion will be sufficient to render it fit enough, without going overboard and to justify that conclusion.

Method of remedy is a matter for the landlord

A landlord is not obliged to carry out the works suggested by the tenant's surveyor. The choice of remedy is for the landlord, absent any self-evident unreasonableness. I would suggest that this effectively boils down to a test of whether the landlord's surveyor's approach is negligent – i.e. something which no reasonably competent surveyor would suggest as a means of remedy.

If it is possible to go into some detail as to alternatives and to discuss why the landlord's approach is better than the claimant's suggestions, this will help the trial judge to decide whether any suggestion by the tenant that the landlord's approach should be rejected.

Cases where a tenant has caused part or all of the damage

Rather than indulging a tenant who has failed to look after the property properly, if there is evidence that the tenant has caused part or all of any damage themselves, this needs to be clearly stated.

Any works necessary as a result of tenant waste or damage should be listed separately and costed. Most landlords do not bother to recharge impecunious tenants but that should not stop a record being made in the report. If appropriate, a counterclaim for the recovery of the cost of remedial works can be made.

Addressing section 11 (3) of the 1985 Act

It is a crucial function of the landlord's surveyor fully to consider the overall standard of repair of the property in accordance with the subsection. I have never seen a tenant's solicitor's surveyor's report address this issue in any more than name. That is partially because few surveyors (who almost invariably practice from the North of England, like their instructing lawyers) are familiar with the housing stock in the local area, so they are unable to comment.

The wording of the statute provides the structure for the assessment and bears constant repetition. The standard of repair is to be determined by reference to the "age, character and prospective life of the dwelling-house and the locality in which it is situated".

This has been addressed earlier in the book, in the context of discussion of the standard necessary. In the preparation of the report, a reasoned, logical approach to each word needs to be taken, and care exercised to be objective and reasonable in the analysis. The judge will be relying on the surveyor's professional ability and knowledge, because the claimant is unlikely to be able to provide any competing opinion.

In most social housing disrepair claims, the standard of the particular property will be higher than that of local privately owned housing stock, whether rented or owner occupied. Private owners are unlikely to have carried out the expensive works necessary to bring the condition of the property up to the DHS. This particularly applies where the property is in a low-income area and the local private landlords struggle to charge sufficient rent.

Using hearsay evidence in the assessment of section 11 (3)

An experienced landlord surveyor will have knowledge of other local housing, or will be able to investigate, either with members of their team or with the Environmental Health team.

Experts are allowed to include in their report the opinions of other experts if their opinion forms a subsidiary part of the necessary material.

If the evidence is hearsay, it is admissible without restriction, provided the requirements of the Civil Evidence Act 1995 are followed. So the evidence needs to be identified as such and the source of the knowledge named.

Such evidence can be obtained from other surveyors, either employed by the landlord, or practising locally. Websites can be used to obtain an idea of the average rent for privately owned housing of a similar type and size.

Assessing the weight of hearsay evidence

The surveyor will need to provide material on the factors set out in section 4 (2) of the Act. It is worth setting those factors out here, so you can understand how easy it is to include hearsay:

> *"(1) In estimating the weight (if any) to be given to hearsay evidence in civil proceedings the court shall have regard to any circumstances from which any inference can reasonably be drawn as to the reliability or otherwise of the evidence.*
>
> *(2) Regard may be had, in particular, to the following—*
>
> > *(a) whether it would have been reasonable and practicable for the party by whom the evidence was adduced to have produced the maker of the original statement as a witness;*
> >
> > *(b) whether the original statement was made contemporaneously with the occurrence or existence of the matters stated;*
> >
> > *(c) whether the evidence involves multiple hearsay;*
> >
> > *(d) whether any person involved had any motive to conceal or misrepresent matters;*
> >
> > *(e) whether the original statement was an edited account, or was made in collaboration with another or for a particular purpose;*
> >
> > *(f) whether the circumstances in which the evidence is adduced as hearsay are such as to suggest an attempt to prevent proper evaluation of its weight."*

Using the evidence for section 11 (3)

The surveyor's evidence on these issues can be determinative of the claim. If there are relatively minor defects, even though they have not been repaired within a reasonable time or to a reasonable standard, it may yet be that the property is not objectively in disrepair, because it is no worse than others in the locality.

Of course, a landlord cannot use its own failure to maintain its stock to a decent level as an excuse and a way of saying that a property in an unacceptable state is nonetheless adequately cared for, so that liability does not arise.

The subsection is intended to protect landlords from the imposition of an unrealistic standard. Few properties will ever be continually in a perfect state of repair. Landlords will inevitably make mistakes, miss appointments or otherwise fail in some way. They should not be held to account by the court for doing so when, overall, they are providing reasonable accommodation at a fair rent.

Report conclusions/summary

The claimant surveyor will invariably have condemned the property, usually for both being out of repair under section 11 and being unfit for human habitation under section 9. On close examination, those assertions may transpire to be untrue.

For instance, a dwelling can be significantly affected by condensation damp, which is caused wholly or mainly by the tenant's own acts or omissions. Yet the surveyor fails to mention the true cause of the problems and blames it instead on matters which the landlord could do something about. So the job of the landlord's surveyor is to be enquiring and objective. They must 'follow the trail' in respect of defects which they see and provide clear reasoned conclusions as to whether they amount to actionable defects or issues for the tenant to resolve themselves.

Often there is an element of both – for instance if a tenant fails to ventilate a property properly, a landlord might put in a whole house ventilation system, at considerable expense, to take the decision out of the tenant's hands. However, tenants have been known to switch these systems off, because they regard them as noisy or wasteful of energy or heat, despite the existence of a heat exchanger.

The landlord's surveyor must not hold back in any opinions, they should provide a foil for the tenant's surveyor's failure to address the issues objectively.

150

Chapter Summary/Key takeaways

- The quality of expert evidence is crucial to the defence of a disrepair claim.

- The Landlord's surveyor will need to produce a report which addresses the issues raised in the claimant surveyor's report, item by item, either admitting responsibility or explaining why liability does not arise.

- Landlord surveyors should be familiar not just with the subject property, but with housing conditions in the area.

- They need to familiarise themselves with common defects, tenant expectations, rent levels and any other factors relevant to the question whether the subject property falls below the standard of others in the locality.

- Following the coming into force of the 2018 Act, they will also need to know about fitness for human habitation.

In the next chapter we look at the drafting of applications for summary judgement/strike out/stay,

CHAPTER SIXTEEN

APPLICATIONS FOR SUMMARY JUDGEMENT / STRIKE OUT / STAY

Just because a claimant issues a claim for damages and an injunction it does not mean that there has to be a trial on the various allegations made, or at least on all of them.

Additionally, the elements of a claim which remain in dispute will have a determinative impact on the track to which the claim is allocated. Finally, a landlord should apply to stay what is left of the claim for ADR, if appropriate.

Time to instruct a lawyer

Once a County Court claim is issued, lawyers will almost inevitably be instructed by landlords. Those lawyers will need to receive at the earliest possible time all the evidence necessary to respond to the claim.

Firms of solicitors who have a specialist housing management team may be able to help with these applications. It is also possible to instruct a barrister directly, without solicitors, provided the landlord has sufficient administrative skills and resources to run the litigation.

Such instructions can be given to barristers under the "Public Access Scheme", a.k.a. "Direct Access". Barristers are obliged to undergo training in handling claims under the scheme and to provide a client Care Letter together with the "Guidance for Lay Clients".

Summary judgement

Through careful analysis of the merits of any disrepair claim, it may be possible to identify elements which patiently obviously have no merit. On those elements the landlord can argue that the claimant ought not to be allowed to pursue the claim to a trial at which the parties would have to give live evidence.

During the early stages of the trial the attention of the court is specifically drawn to the availability of summary judgement, by PD 26, para 5. that says that *"part of the court's duty of active case management is the summary disposal of issues which do not need full investigation and trial"* (rule 1.4 (2) (c)).

That can include strike out or summary judgement and the court can use the powers either on an application or on its own initiative. If the case for striking out or entering summary judgement against a claimant on a claim for specific performance is sufficiently clear, it may be possible to persuade the court to strike it out at the allocation hearing, without an application.

But in most cases, this is unlikely to find favour with a busy District Judge, as the claimant will urge the court not to make such an important decision summarily.

No judgement in default pending hearing of summary judgement/strike out application

Judgement in default of service of a Defence cannot be entered against a defendant who has issued an application to strike out a claim or for summary judgement-CPR 12.3 (3) (a) and the application has not been disposed of. This is important-if the application for summary judgement/strike out is issued when the claim is received, much work can be saved. This can have a significant effect on the complexity of the pleadings, particularly if it is possible to strike out or enter summary judgement against the claimant on the claim for specific performance.

Mechanics of the application

There is plenty of law on summary judgement applications. CPR 24 deals with the mechanics of the application and the test which needs to be met by the N244 application notice and the witness statement in support.

An application can be brought if the landlord can show that there is no "realistic" as opposed to a "fanciful" prospect of success[28]. It must be "more than merely arguable".[29]

The court must not conduct a "mini trial", but "*this does not mean that the court must take at face value and without analysis everything that a claimant says in his statements before the court. In some cases it may be clear that there is no real substance in factual assertions made, particularly if contradicted by contemporaneous documents.*"

The law is set out in the White Book and in drafting the evidence in support careful attention needs to be paid to the exact reasons why the claim is hopeless.

In reaching its conclusion the court must take into account not just the evidence before it in the application but also any evidence which can reasonably be expected to be available if the claim goes to trial[30]. So it is important to anticipate what a claimant may say in response to the application.

Applications in respect of unnecessary claims for specific performance

The most obvious target for an application for summary judgement is the claim for a mandatory injunction for specific performance. There is much case law on the subject, but essentially such relief is intended for serious cases where a defendant needs to be forced by the court to comply with its obligations.

Bearing in mind that such injunctions are enforceable by imprisonment, it is obvious that in the vast majority of social housing disrepair claims, injunctive relief is totally inappropriate.

The promise of a social landlord that it will carry out repairs within a certain period of time should be enough to dispose of that aspect of the

---

[28] see the case of *Swain v Hillman* [2001] 1 All ER 91

[29] *ED & F Man Liquid Products v Patel* [2003] EW Civ 472 at [8]

[30] see *Royal Brompton Hospital NHS Trust V Hammond (No. 5) EWCA Civ 550*

claim. But it is far better to have carried out the works by the date of the summary judgement hearing.

Strike out under CPR 3.4

Sometimes claims are so poorly pleaded that an application to strike out the particulars of claim can be included in the application for summary judgement. The applicant will need to prove one of the three conditions in CPR 3.4 (2).

A particularly poorly pleaded set of particulars of claim might generate an application to strike out, or at least to strike out certain parts of the POC.

Equally, if a pleading relies on an expert's report that on examination contains no allegations of disrepair (for instance a report where the only defect is condensation and the only works recommended involve telling the tenant to ventilate better and carrying out a mould wash) it may be possible to persuade the court to strike out the claim as well as entering summary judgement against the claimant. But generally, the remedy of summary judgement will suffice.

At one point district judges were striking out disrepair claims for the claimant's failure to comply with a rule/practice direction because they had failed to agree to ADR. It is still worth asking the court to do so where there has been a serious breach of the provisions on ADR, perhaps when the claimant totally ignores the invitations and does not even answer the request made in the response to the letter of claim.

The applicant also needs to state that there is "no other compelling reason for a trial".

The best time to make the application is before or at the same time as directions questionnaires are filed. But summary judgement application can even be made at trial.

Stay for ADR

Additionally, in certain circumstances, the court will stay a claim to allow the parties to engage in alternative dispute resolution. While the landlord will suggest that should take place through its complaints process, the tenant's solicitors invariably criticise that proposed method and ask for a joint settlement meeting.

CPR 26.4 provides that a party in filing the directions questionnaire can make a written request for is to be stayed for ADR, in which case the court will stay for a period of one month.

Alternatively, by CPR 26.4 (2A), "*if the court otherwise considers that such a state would be appropriate, the court will direct that proceedings either in whole or in part, be stayed for one month or for such other period as it considers appropriate. By sub-rule (3) "the court may extend the stay until such date or for such specified period as it considers appropriate.*"

So the CPR expressly provide for a compulsory stay of the proceedings, if the court considers that it would be appropriate. Unless a claimant can show that they have already tried the formal complaints process and have not gained satisfaction, it is difficult to see how a claimant tenant could be prejudiced by such a compulsory stay, provided that it does not delay the claim unduly.

The stay can be ordered for only a month, or for a longer period. Two or three months will provide sufficient time for the whole complaints process to be exhausted.

The law behind the application to stay

There is much in the White Book on ADR – see Volume 2, section 14. It describes ADR as "*an integral part of the litigation process.*" The Access to Justice Interim Report said that the range and availability of ADR procedures should be increased and that the use of ADR by parties had been encouraged by the court in various ways.

The case law

Although the case of *Halsey v Milton Keynes General NHS Trust* [2004] EWCA Civ 576 held that parties could not be forced to mediate, in other cases some courts have taken the view that they have power to direct mediation – see the case of *Honda v Neeson* [2009] EWHC 1213, in which the Judge said "*In summary then, I shall dismiss the application and direct that both parties use their best endeavours to ensure that a mediation is heard before (date)".*

Other pertinent cases include *PDF II SA v OMF Co-1 Ltd* [2013] EWCA Civ 1288 *and Jet 2 Holidays Ltd v Hughes* [2019] EWCA Civ 1858 and many others listed in the White Book at section 14-2. Now that the court has a duty actively to case manage, there are various arguments which can be raised in support of the contention that a stay can be ordered despite one party objecting-see the commentary in the White Book at section 14-6.

See also *Uren v Corporate Leisure (UK) Ltd* [2011] EWCA Civ 66 and the other cases listed in the White Book at 14-7. That concludes by saying that the issue of compulsory mediation "*is one therefore that is likely to be, or at the least ought to be, reconsidered by the Court of Appeal or the Civil Procedure Rule Committee. No doubt when it is reconsidered the approach taken by the court of justice of the European Union, which held that in certain circumstances compulsory mediation was permissible, will be taken into account*".

Cases involving public authorities

In *R. (Cowl) v Plymouth City Council* [2001] EWCA Civ 1935 the Court of Appeal said that in disputes between public authorities and members of the public for whom they are responsible, insufficient attention was being paid to the paramount importance of saving costs and reducing delay by avoiding recourse to the application to the judicial review procedure. The court was enjoined to use its powers to ensure that the parties tried to resolve their dispute with the minimum involvement of the court. That could involve telling the parties that they had to attend a hearing at which they would be asked to explain what steps they had taken to use ADR.

Additionally, you can now cite the decision of the single judge in *Hockett* to the effect that legal proceedings should not be instituted prior to an attempt ADR through the complaints process.

Recent cases

The case of *Lomax v Lomax* [2019] EWCA Civ 1467 (Court of Appeal) supports the proposition advanced that the judicial attitude to compulsory ADR has developed since Halsey v Milton Keynes), so that the Court may in appropriate cases require the parties to attempt it, without the consent of one or even both of them.

Although that case concerned Early Neutral Evaluation, other forms of ADR were discussed [para 29, per Moylan LJ] without distinction. There is no distinction for these purposes between ENE, FDR and ADR in the PAP approved mode, and a formal complaints process.

In the context of PAD applications, in *Wimpey Homes UK Ltd v Harron Homes [2020] EWHC 1120 (TCC)*, Fraser J dismissed a PAD application because the respondent sought ADR through the means of expert determination and the applicant had refused. He held that the fact that ADR had been rejected was material. In a case where a party has sought to refer the dispute to ADR, there is a question whether the disclosure stage will ever be reached, although whether such issues are questions of threshold or discretion is arguable.

He cited *Hutchison 3G v O2* [2008], in which the Court reminded itself that PAD is appropriate only where the circumstances are outside "the usual run" to allow the hurdle to be surmounted of showing that it is necessary because it would be useful in achieving a settlement or otherwise saving costs. He also referred to *Birse Construction Ltd v HLC Engenharia SA* [2006] EWHC 1258 (TCC) saying that disclosure before the proper time is not something which should be lightly ordered in cases where disclosure is a labour-intensive exercise and a major head of costs.

Most important, he said that ADR has "*a vast number of advantages to parties to commercial agreements*" and "It is almost always far quicker than litigation, and almost always far cheaper, to have disputes resolved in this way. The court in all cases will be astute to prevent pre-action disclosure being used either to frustrate, impede or interfere with contractually agreed ADR mechanisms."

The court should be reminded that litigation can cause significant damage to the relationship between a landlord and tenant by contested litigation, whichever party wins. It is therefore in the interests of justice to discourage litigation between parties who will have to continue to deal with each other whatever the result – see *Shirayama Shokusan v Danovo Ltd* [2003] EWHC 3006 (Ch), in which the Court also held that the Court could stay the proceedings for the parties to mediate – the case was decided before *Halsey*.

This argument has found favour with District Judges for many years, but has recently been disapproved of by a County Court judge, who said that the tenancy did not contain a term requiring tenants to attempt ADR before litigating, so the court would not dismiss a PAD application for that reason. The same reasoning would apply to an application to stay.

The Solicitors' Handbook and Code of Conduct 2011The mainstay of the application is the law relating to paragraph 4.1 of the Protocol and the relevant provisions of the CPR and the Pre-Action Protocol, as discussed earlier in the book.

There is also an obligation under the Solicitors Handbook and Code of Conduct 2011, which requires solicitors to "consider all options" for their clients. There are no specific requirements but outcome O (1.12) does require that *'clients are in a position to make informed decisions about the services they need, how their matter will be handled and the options available to them'* and this must be construed to include discussing with them the options available to resolve the dispute without litigation.

Although it is worth mentioning, it does not add much to the now substantial body of law giving the court the opportunity to stay for ADR.

Preparing an application to stay the claim for ADR

It is necessary to compile a witness statement which deals with the enormous cost in terms of officer time and public funds which disrepair claims generate. That can be supplemented by information about the number of claims made in the past and the number being received at the present time. It is also possible to get figures from other social landlords about how many claims they are experiencing. The overall message is that these claims are disproportionate and should not be allowed to go to court unless the parties have attempted ADR.

Obviously, the cost-free version, in the form of the complaints process, is preferable. If that does not work, the parties can try other types of ADR, but mediation and joint settlement meetings are likely to be very expensive because the tenant's lawyers will be involved.

Requests for further information to supplement applications

When investigating the merits of the claim it may be necessary to tie the claimant to their case and ensure that no further arguments will come out of the woodwork when making the application for summary judgement/strike out.

Requests for further information are made under CPR 18 and need to be made under the procedure in PD 18. First the party making the request must serve a written request for clarification or information, giving a date by which the response should be served, which must be a reasonable time hence.

Brief requests can be made by letter, more complex requests should be made in a separate document. The maker must state that they are making a Request under Part 18 and they should deal with the other matters set out in CPR PD 18.1.6.

Replies to requests

Responses must be in writing, dated and signed by the party providing the information with a Statement of Truth. This is important, as a claimant can be reminded in cross-examination that any answers given in their Part 18 Replies were provided in the knowledge that they could be sent to prison if they knowingly misstated a fact.

If replies are not provided

If objection is taken to answering the questions or to doing so within the time allowed, a response must be given, whereupon the party requesting will have to make an application to the court under Part 18, for which the procedure is set out in 18 PD.5. That will need to be served on the other side.

If the recipient does not reply, the maker of the request issues an application which need only contain a brief statement in box 10 of the N244 that a request has been made and not answered. They need not serve the application on the other party (CPR PD 18 5.5 (1)).

The court will then make an order without a hearing, provided at least 14 days have passed since the Request was served and the time allowed for a response has expired.

Requests for specific dates on which notice is said to have been given

It is particularly important to use this procedure to force the tenant to commit to dates of notice alleged to have been given, or to elicit a concession that they cannot provide any dates.

The tenant will have to answer the Request with a signed Statement of Truth. Once a tenant has said that they cannot be more specific, their witness statement should not contain any allegations that they gave notice on specific dates and in court they can be cross-examined if they then unexpectedly remember dates.

Request for information on alleged loss and damage

If the claim for loss and damage is broadly pleaded, or personal injury is alleged without a medical report being provided, a request can be made to particularise the alleged damage and application can be made for summary judgement on the personal injury claim if no medical report is served.

Preparing an application for summary judgement/strike out

Lawyers working for landlords will already have at their disposal their surveyor's report, which will have appended to it the full Repairs History for the relevant period, together with the Scott Schedule.

There are two areas of attack open to a landlord: (1) the claim for an injunction and (2) the claim for damages.

Asking the court to dismiss the application for an injunction

The first and most important target is the application for a mandatory injunction for specific performance of the repairing covenant. An order for specific performance is supported by an injunction, which is backed up by the threat of imprisonment.

There are very few landlords who positively refuse to carry out repairs. It is inappropriate for social landlords employees to face imprisonment for failing to ensure that repairs are carried out, except perhaps in exceptional circumstances.

Often the landlord's surveyor will agree to a greater or lesser extent with the findings of a tenant's surveyor in respect of the existence of defects. In respect of every defect which is agreed to exist and for which a remedy is proposed, the landlord can argue that there is no dispute between the parties on either issue. It follows from that position that the court is entitled to find that there is no dispute on the point which needs to be determined at a trial.

In respect of application for an injunction, this goes to the heart of the claim. If a claim for disrepair does not include a justifiable request for a mandatory injunction, it is likely to be allocated to the Small Claims Track. We will address those issues in the next chapter in the context of allocation to track.

Challenging the value of the claim during the application

Tenants will invariably frame the claim in the LOC and POC as having a starting date of the beginning of the tenancy. Often it is alleged that defects were already present when the tenant moved into the property.

Such claims are subject to challenge, because the pre-letting/void survey will often record, with photographic evidence, the condition and state of repair before the arrival of the tenant.

Responding to a claim for damages framed in the usual wide and all-encompassing way demands attention to detail and a careful investigation of each of the allegations, so that they can be shown to be wholly or partly misconceived.

163

Addressing allocation in the application for summary judgement

There will be instances where even though there might remain after summary judgement a valid claim for specific performance, but the outstanding defects are so minor that the works will cost less than £1,000, and the period of claim is so short or the historic loss of amenity is so minor that it should be obvious to the court that the claim for damages will not exceed £1,000.

It is the cost of the works according to the landlord's repairs team which is relevant, not the cost as estimated by the claimant's surveyor. In this regard it is helpful if the landlord can justify their assessment of the cost of works, by reference to their schedule of rates or any other credible evidence.

In many cases, the court will agree that the hearing that after entering summary judgement on part of the claim, the remainder of the claim should be allocated to the Small Claims Track

Evidence-the tenancy file

Useful information and evidence can often be found in the tenancy file. Sometimes there are reports in the file which relates to repairs and provide facts which can be used in the explanation of the history of a defect or a repair.

Alternatively, the file might show occasional or frequent contact with no mention of repairs issues. Most social landlords will require their housing officers to pass on reports of disrepair, or have a policy that they must tell the tenant to use the disrepair call centre or report online.

Individual recollection

Sometimes individual surveyors, housing officers or other employees will be familiar with the property and its repairs history, or they will know other helpful information about the tenant. The landlord's response policy for disrepair claims should provide for information gathering from any individual who may be able to help.

Collation of evidence and assessment of liability

The material obtained from the various sources can be presented to the court as a surveyor's report and possibly additionally, as a witness statement, for instance when a housing officer knows a substantial amount about the tenant. The conclusions reached will determine whether an application for summary judgement should be made and, if so, in respect of which parts of the claim. Lawyers involved in these claims will be familiar with the drafting of such applications. The aim is to dispose of the injunction claim as a minimum, on the basis that the landlord has never refused to do works and a claim for specific performance is inappropriate.

A decision then has to be made on whether there is any arguable claim and, if so, which defects over what period of time.

Landlords with broken repairs systems

Occasionally, a social landlord will face such technical and operational difficulties that the repairs system ceases to function properly and wholesale delays occur. The difficulties caused by the pandemic being such an example.

Social landlords will have long delays in the programming of routine repairs. This does not mean that the court should impose an injunction against employees requiring them to repair or face imprisonment. If works are ordered but cannot be done within a reasonable time and the tenant continues to suffer loss of amenity, the remedy should sound in damages at the most. Unless the landlord refuses to repair, the court should not impose an injunction.

Content of the N244 application form

A decision must be made as to which parts of the claim are to be attacked and which allowed to continue to trial. Sometimes the entire claim can be attacked, if the documentary evidence is good enough. Often it will be the application for an injunction which is the best target. In some (unusual) cases, it may not be appropriate to make an application for summary judgement at all.

Occasionally an application can be combined with an application to strike out the claim as an abuse of process. This might be appropriate where a tenant has behaved in a way which is clearly and seriously in breach of the CPR, or of the Pre-Action Protocol.

There are specific requirements of an application for summary judgement, and it is important to get the procedural aspects right.

The application notice will contain the orders sought, the reasons for asking the court to make them (in box 3), and the bare bones of the evidence (in box 10). The surveyor's report and, if drafted, the additional witness evidence will be attached.

Conduct of the hearing

It is wise to prepare a skeleton argument, setting out the basis on which the application is pursued. Some district judges will be familiar with such claims, but most will need help when it comes to disrepair/unfitness law.

The idea of compulsory stay for ADR is also novel to some judges, at least at present

Review of the application before the hearing

The decision whether to make the application should be reviewed when, or if the claimant files evidence in response. It is necessary to keep an open mind on the issue, encase the tenant adduces evidence which could cause the application to fail.

Chapter summary/key takeaways

- The availability of the remedy of summary judgement/strike out/stay is a powerful weapon in the armoury of a social landlord, provided that they know when and how should be used.

- Such applications require careful planning and collection of evidence if they are to succeed. Most social landlords will have records which are sufficiently detailed to provide them with an opportunity to rebut much of what a tenant says.

- An application can be made simply to stay the claim for ADR, or to seek summary judgement or strike out on part or all of the claim, and a stay of the remainder. That hearing might also deal with allocation, which is addressed in chapter 18.

The next chapter considers the drafting of the Defence. If an application has been made for summary judgement/strike out, this should not be attempted before the landlord knows which parts of the claim are left in contention. This leads to reduced legal fees.

CHAPTER SEVENTEEN

DRAFTING THE DEFENCE

The Defence gives the landlord an opportunity to take issue with the various respects in which disrepair claims are usually defective or lacking.

Time for filing the Defence

The acknowledgement of service must be filed within 14 days after service of the claim form if the particulars of claim come it, or within 14 days of service of the POC if they are not served contemporaneously.

Provided that a defendant has filed an acknowledgement of service under CPR 10, the Defence has to be filed and served 28 days after service of the particulars of claim, which themselves must be either served with the claim form or within 14 days after service.

If the Defendant fails to file an acknowledgement of service, they only have 14 days in which to serve the Defence. It follows that it is important to serve that acknowledgement of service in every case.

That time limit does not give a landlord very long to gather the information necessary to plead the Defence properly. Fortunately, in most cases, the pre-litigation skirmish will have meant that most of the relevant information is to hand, and the pleading can be done relatively swiftly.

If it turns out not to be possible to file the Defence within the time limit, most claimant solicitors will allow extra time for the preparation of a Defence if requested. The parties can agree an extension of up to 28 days between themselves.

If the claimant does refuse to give such an extension, the court will usually exercise its discretion in favour of extending time, provided good reason can be given for the delay.

No Defence need be filed in some circumstances

As I have already said, if you are making an application for summary judgement/strike out Defence-relying on CPR 12.3.

The mechanics of serving a Defence

CPR 15 contains the rules as to when a Defence must be filed and what it should contain. Disrepair claims will almost inevitably involve disputes as to the facts, so they will have been issued under Part 7 rather than Part 8. If a claimant uses the Part 8 procedure, the defendant should not follow the rules in CPR 15.

Counterclaims

It is sometimes necessary to include a counterclaim against a tenant, particularly if they have caused substantial damage to the property.

Reply to the Defence

Most Defences are met with a Reply. It is up to the claimant to file their Reply with the Directions Questionnaire and to serve it on the defendant at the same time it is filed. The parties are not allowed to exchange any further pleadings without permission of the court.

This means that all the issues must be raised in those three preliminary documents.

The parties can amend their existing statements of case. The normal order for costs on any amendment is that the party making the changes pays the costs of and occasioned by those changes.

The content of a Defence

A defendant landlord will need to plead in the Defence all the facts on which they rely, but not the law. It is very long as I have tried to anticipate as many issues in the claim as possible. I

The best way to approach the content of the Defence is to give an example of what might be included in such a document, so I have included one as an appendix.

Chapter summary/key takeaways

- If no application for summary judgement or strike out has been made, the Defence has to be drafted.

- In a disrepair claim the Defence can be lengthy and reasonably complex, and you probably will need lawyers to prepare it.

In the next chapter we will look at transfer and allocation to track, and in particular the importance of the Small Claims Track in disrepair claims.

CHAPTER EIGHTEEN

TRANSFER AND ALLOCATION TO TRACK

Transfer to the defendant's home court

Often claimant solicitors issue disrepair claims in their home court, or even in other courts which have no apparent connection to either party.

Landlords should ensure that the court transfers the claim to their home court, either using CPR 30.3 or if it has been issued as a money claim, by telling the court as soon the claim is issued that it should be transferred pursuant to CPR 26.2A (2) and in the case of a claim for damages and an injunction, under sub-rule (4) or (5).

There is no automatic transfer to the defendant's home court if they are a company or a corporation, so landlords need to ensure that transfer happens. If it is only an interim matter with which the court is dealing (e.g. pre-action disclosure), it may be reluctant to transfer the claim before hearing.

Criteria for transfers

The relevant criteria in CPR 30.2 (2) are:

> "(a) the financial value of the claim and the amount in dispute, if different;
>
> (b) whether it would be more convenient or fair for hearings (including the trial) to be held in some other court;
>
> (c) the availability of a judge specialising in the type of claim in question and in particular the availability of a specialist judge sitting in an appropriate regional specialist court;

(d) whether the facts, legal issues, remedies or procedures involved are simple or complex;

(e) the importance of the outcome of the claim to the public in general;

(f) the facilities available to the court at which the claim is being dealt with, particularly in relation to –

(i) any disabilities of a party or potential witness;

(ii) … "

If a substantive claim has been issued, the court will transfer to the hearing centre in which the property is situated at the earliest possible moment.

Allocation to track

Claimant lawyers will be primarily interested in the potential for the recovery of costs. They work on conditional fee agreements and the track to which a claim is allocated by the court can have a fundamental effect on the pursuit of the claim, as claimant solicitors will not wish to pursue claims on the Small Claims Track ("SCT"). There is much greater potential for them to recover costs on the Fast Track ("FT") but there are still significant restraints on the quantum of those costs.

Costs on the multi-track ("MT") are not so limited and can rapidly become very substantial. Allocation to the MT has very substantial costs implications for both parties. There will be few disrepair claims which could ever be valuable and complex enough for the parties to contemplate allocation to the MT. In my view it is to be avoided, if possible, unless the landlord is wholly confident of winning at trial and recovering its costs.

Therefore, this chapter concentrates on the choice between the SCT and the FT. My preference is that claims should be dealt with in the SCT, where the implications for both parties are far less serious in terms of costs and hearings will be listed much more swiftly, with a minimum of unnecessary preparation. This saves both landlords significant investment in legal fees and officer time and further, it is less stressful for all involved.

In very few, rare cases, the claim for damages and an injunction is patiently so modest that the case is obviously suitable for the SCT.

Alternatively, the landlord may be able to show using a surveyor's report, invoices and possibly even a certificate signed by the tenant, that no works remain outstanding, so SCT trial is appropriate provided the claim for damages is less than £1,000. Alternatively, after an application for summary judgement, if it is evident that little remains in dispute, it may be appropriate to allocate the SCT.

The process of allocation to track

Upon the filing of a Defence, a court officer will provisionally decide the most suitable track for the claim and serve a notice of proposed allocation under CPR 26.3 (1). It is then up to the parties to decide whether the track decision suits them, or whether they should apply to have the claim allocated to a different track. The court may ask for further information on allocation, which has to be provided within 14 days (para 4.2 (2)).

Alternatively, upon the filing of Allocation Questionnaires pursuant to CPR 26.5 (1) (a) the landlord can request allocation to the SCT, while the tenant's solicitor will ask for allocation to the FT.

The process of decision-making on allocation is set out in CPR 26 and its PD, at PD 26 4.1. The court will generally give brief reasons for an allocation decision, except when all parties agree on allocation.

The importance of allocation to track

Cases which are listed in the SCT will not usually result in any significant award of costs against a party unless they can be shown to have behaved unreasonably or dishonestly. So claimant solicitors will not be able to recover the substantial sums which they claim in FT trials. But proceeding on the SCT also means that a landlord who wins at trial will not get its costs back, in normal circumstances.

Even in cases allocated to the FT, issues of proportionality and fixed fees for the barrister's appearance limit the amount of costs recoverable in the event of the successful pursuit of a claim to trial.

Financial limits for tracking of disrepair claims

A disrepair claim will normally be allocated to the Small Claims Track unless it includes a claim for a mandatory injunction and either the cost of works necessary is over £1,000, or the damages reasonably sought are likely to be more than £1,000. A claim made only for damages for disrepair will usually be allocated to the SCT unless it exceeds £10,000.

CPR 26.1 addresses allocation. The rules provide that tracking must reflect the time and resources appropriate for the just disposal of a case at proportionate cost. It is important to understand the principles behind the crucial question of tracking.

Rule 1.1 sets out the overriding objective of the CPR, which are a new procedural code enabling the court to deal with cases justly and at proportionate cost. CPR 1.1(2) provides that dealing with a case justly and at proportionate cost includes, so far as is practicable:

(a) ensuring that the parties are on an equal footing;

(b) saving expense;

(c) dealing with the case in ways which are proportionate –

(i) to the amount of money involved;

(ii) to the importance of the case;

(iii) to the complexity of the issues; and

(iv) to the financial position of each party;

(d) ensuring that it is dealt with expeditiously and fairly;

(e) allotting to it an appropriate share of the court's resources, while taking into account the need to allot resources to other cases; and

(f) enforcing compliance with rules, practice directions and orders.

The proportionality of the claim has been a consideration since April 2013, when court was specifically enjoined to consider that issue in case management decisions. That has a clear and direct impact on the need to encourage claimant tenants to use a cost-free complaints process

General rule for allocation:

This is set out in CPR 26. CPR 26.7 (1) says:

> (1) *In considering whether to allocate a claim to the normal track for that claim under rule 26.6, the court will have regard to the matters mentioned in rule 26.8(1).*

Rule 26.8(1) follows:

> *Matters relevant to allocation to a track*
>
> *(1) When deciding the track for a claim, the matters to which the court shall have regard include –*
>
>> *(a) the financial value, if any, of the claim;*
>>
>> *(b) …*
>>
>> *(c) the likely complexity of the facts, law or evidence;…*
>>
>>> *(i)   the circumstances of the parties.*

See also CPR 26.8 and the allocation principles set out in PD 26.7 26 which supplements CPR Part 26.

Matters relevant to allocation

Usually, the first consideration on allocation is the value of the sum in dispute. In determining the value of a claim, interest, costs and *any amount not in dispute* are not included in the assessment. *"Any amount not in dispute"* includes an admission made by the defendant prior to allocation which reduces the amount in dispute. Cf *Akhtar v Boland* [2014] EWCA Civ 872, paragraphs 22 and 23.

Although there is nothing in the CPR which deals with admissions that works are accepted as needing to be carried out, paragraph 7.4(4) of PD

26 says, "*It follows from these provisions that if, in relation to a claim the value of which is above the small claims track limit of £10,000, the defendant makes, before allocation, an admission that reduces the amount in dispute to a figure below £10,000 (see CPR Part 14), the normal track for the claim will be the small claims track*".

Allocation in housing disrepair claims

Disrepair claims should not be allocated to the small claims track if they involve a claim for an injunction and either that claim or the claim for damages is valued at more than £1,000. The notes say:

> "*Housing disrepair—any claim which includes a claim by a tenant of residential premises against a landlord where the tenant seeks an order requiring the landlord to carry out repairs or other work and the costs of that are estimated to be no more than £1,000. This applies even if some other remedy is also sought in the same claim as long as it is also not more than £1,000 (CPR 26.6(1)(b)).*"

However if the issue is marginal, there is leeway provided by the rules themselves: "*Even if the claim exceeds the limit, the court can allocate the claim to the small claims track (CPR PD 26, para 8.1(2))*".

Requesting allocation or reallocation to the SCT

CPR 26 on allocation specifies how the landlord should go about first asking for allocation to the SCT. When filling in the response to the claim and/or the DQ, the landlord will want to make it plain that they seek allocation to the SCT. If the court allocates the claim to track, it will serve a notice of allocation on the parties pursuant to CPR 26.9.

If the court allocates track of its own motion, a party may seek reallocation under CPR 26.10 if they believe the case has been wrongly tracked by the court officer. So the question of which track is appropriate can be determined at a hearing upon the request of a party dissatisfied with the allocation.

Preparing to argue the question of allocation

The landlord's surveyor will need to address the question of what works have been carried out and what remains outstanding. Obviously, it is best to be able to prove that there are no works at all outstanding. Otherwise, the landlord will need to establish that both the claim for damages should be valued at less than £1,000 and there is less than £1,000 worth of work outstanding. If either of those heads of claim exceed that figure, the court will allocate to the FT.

Where there is no genuine claim for specific performance

A disrepair claim will be allocated to the SCT if the claimant cannot show that there is a genuine claim for specific performance of the contract and the damages expected are less than £10,000.

The primary argument of tenants is that there is a genuine claim for specific performance. This is often untrue. An application for specific performance is ultimately enforced by injunctive relief, which carries a possible penalty of imprisonment. Case law has established that it should be granted only in exceptional cases. That is obviously right – it would be wrong in principle to expose ordinary employees of a social landlord repairs team to the threat of imprisonment simply because subcontractors on a job fail to turn up and carry out works.

In almost every social housing case there is no need for the claimant to apply in the first place for specific performance. Social landlords do not deliberately refuse to carry out repairs. There can be circumstances in which there are delays, or repairs to a particular defect are cancelled (particularly where a tenant is out when contractors call and does not subsequently contact the landlord again).

But when told that the tenant is unhappy with the state of repair of the property, most social landlords will get on and inspect, then repair. Often works are carried out very shortly after the claim is intimated.

To recap, provided the result is that the tenant stops suffering any significant loss of amenity, the choice of works is that of the landlord and not the tenant. So claimant lawyers should not succeed in an argument that their surveyors says that the roof should be replaced rather than

179

patched, provided the patching provides satisfactory protection from the elements (see the facts of the *Trustees of Dame Hungerford* case.

Gaining access to do works-injunctions

The Protocol requires tenants in paragraph 7.6 to allow landlords access to carry out works and there are no exceptions specified. Previously many tenant solicitors used to advise their clients not to allow a landlord in to do the works, particularly before they had sent a surveyor in to inspect.

It is incumbent on the tenant solicitors to get the survey done quickly, and they should not use that excuse to prevent access. Delay in the works can increase the amount of damages payable, as the tenant will argue that although they had refused access, the landlord could have forced entry using their legal right if they chose to do so.

Therefore, any refusal of access by the tenant must be dealt with swiftly, by a written warning and either forced entry if the tenancy provides for it, or by application for an access injunction.

If there are any works necessary to remedy defects which threaten the health and safety of the tenant, occupant or others, an application can be made under the Antisocial Behaviour Crime and Policing Act 2014.

Otherwise, the injunctive relief needs to be sought under the terms of the tenancy, using the Part 8 procedure.

Evidencing the costs in a disrepair claim allocated to the FT

As part of the evidence in the allocation hearing, the landlord will need to show that costs after trials in the FT are disproportionate to the sums involved. This is invariably true. Even if a claimant tenant's costs are only £15,000, if the tenant recovers £2,000 in damages, this is wholly disproportionate to the amount at stake.

But tenant solicitors more usually claim between £25,000 and £35,000 in costs at trial. Clearly there will be few cases in which such costs are proportionate. Admissible evidence needs to be produced to the court of those likely costs, in the form of a witness statement by the landlord or their solicitor.

Costs when repairs have been done

As I have already said in Chapter 10,, landlord representatives must read *Birmingham City Council v Lee* to learn about what happens to the costs in such cases. There is a significant amount in the judgement concerning whether costs should be awarded on the FastTrack basis even though there are no repairs to be done.

The question is whether the claim is brought in circumstances which *justified* the institution of proceedings. Much of the time landlords should argue that the claim should never have been capable of allocation to the FastTrack because they did not refuse to carry out works once they became aware of the need to do so.

It is necessary to make the court aware of these issues when addressing allocation.

Usually, when a claim is allocated to track, pursuant to CPR 44.9 (2) the special rules about SCT and FT costs apply to the period before as well as after allocation, unless the court or a practice direction provides otherwise. There is an exception in CPR 44.11 when the court has already made an order in relation to costs before allocation takes place. That order is not affected by the subsequently allocation.

The PAP provides in paragraph 3.7 (echoing *Birmingham v Lee*) that "(a) *If the tenant's claim is settled without litigation on terms which justify bringing it, the landlord will pay the tenant's reasonable costs or out of pocket expenses...*". The Guidance Note 4.2 (b) says that most cases are likely to fall within the FastTrack, at which the Protocol is aimed.

A claimant can argue that they should be entitled to an order for costs on the FastTrack basis up until the date on which works were carried out. But to achieve that order at trial, the claimant will need to be able to prove that the landlord had constructive or actual notice of the particular defects repaired and that the landlord failed to repair within a reasonable time, and that the repairs which the landlord was refusing to carry out were valued at more than £1000 when it became necessary to involve lawyers.

Of course often it will be argued that, as the complaints process resolve matters without the involvement of any lawyers, any costs incurred by them prior to the complaint decision are not recoverable.

Most of the time, on careful analysis of the facts, tenants cannot do justify allocation to the FT. Further, for the purposes of allocation, any amount which is not in dispute is to be excluded from consideration when allocating to track. Therefore, if a landlord admits that certain works were necessary and (if appropriate) that they had not been carried out for a particular period of time, the amount of damages payable in respect of that element of the claim is omitted and the claim allocated according to the remainder in dispute.

Those handling disrepair claims will be familiar with figures like this-they form the basis of my wish that social landlords should face fewer disrepair claims.

Other arguments for allocation of disrepair claims to the SCT

In disrepair claims, apart from the expected value of the claim, there are likely to be two arguments raised on the part of claimants: the claim is too complex to be dealt with in the SCT and there is an inequality of arms if the claimant does not have the services of a lawyer. The proportionality of costs will also be relevant. Both of these can be defeated.

In two cases on the complex area of PPI law, judges have made observations which are helpful to landlords in disrepair claims: *Gillies v Blackhorse Limited* [2011] EW Misc 20 (19 December 2011) and *Loughlin v Blackhorse Limited* [2012] EW Misc 8 (CC) (13 January 2012). They were both appeals against the allocation of a claim to the SCT.

The claimants relied on the complexity of the facts and the law and on the parties' circumstances as they argued there should be equality of arms by providing for legal representation for both. Both appeals addressed the issues in the same way. The court held that it is actual complexity, rather than 'ostensible' complexity with which the court is concerned.

I will address each in turn.

Complexity

There is nothing in the principles listed in CPR PD 26.7 to provide guidance on how to judge complexity. The central allegation in both PPI claims was one of misrepresentation, although a variety of different legal claims were pleaded, in a similar way to disrepair claims, in which the central allegations is a failure to repair within a reasonable time, put under multiple heads of claim.

In *Gillies*, the judge noted that, said that:

> "*Mr Gillies' claim is based on a number of familiar grounds; he alleges (amongst other things) misrepresentation, breach of the Insurance Conduct of Business Rules amounting to a breach of statutory duty under Section 150 of the Financial Services and Markets Act 2000, an unfair relationship pursuant to the Consumer Credit Act, negligence and breach of contract. Those are all certainly pleaded allegations and they are issues raised in many of these cases*".

In both cases, the court observed that the law had been carefully considered in the appeal courts. In *Loughlin*, the judge considered that, "*These matters are much more straightforward than they appear to be…Looking at the pleadings some of them have now been dealt with at a higher level ……… and the district judge is well able to take those matters into account in guiding the litigant through the small claim*".

Cases allocated to the SCT can involve complex issues and the court should not allocate to the FT on the assumption that any complex issues must be dealt with on that track. Again, in *Loughlin* the judge said, "*it is my experience of experienced district judges that, in dealing with these cases which are the subject of a significant number of claims, they become pretty experienced in the issues that arise and how to deal with them, and if something goes wrong then the litigant may appeal*".

in *Williams v Santander UK Plc* [2015] EW Misc B37 (CC) (21 August 2015) the court heard an application to re-allocate to the FT a case which had been allocated to the SCT. The claimant argued that it should be FT because of legal complexity and the inequality of arms.

As to inequality of arms, the district judge hearing the application for reallocation noted that *"…the court is and, as judges, we are, regularly faced with litigants in person and we try to ensure at all costs that the parties are helped through any difficulties that they may face in such a hearing"*.

Equality of arms

Litigants in person in the SCT are protected by the overriding objective, which imposes an obligation on the court to ensure procedural fairness for all parties and to allow a degree of latitude to litigants in person.

In *Loughlin*, the judge accepted that if the case was allocated to the SCT, it was likely that the claimant would have to bring his case on his own (with Black Horse likely to be represented by lawyers) but said:

> *"….given that the issues in this case are relatively straightforward and more or less the same issues as arise in Gillies, it does not seem to me that there is any real justification that this point is a good one. The real question here is whether this is a case which should be allocated to the small claim or the fast track in order to enable there to be a fuller argument by legal representation of the issues that arise"*.

Proportionality of costs

Costs must be proportionate to the matters in issue. In *Williams v Santander*, the District Judge responsible for the initial allocation to the small claims track noted in his order that *"the costs likely to be incurred by allocation to any other track would be wholly disproportionate to the sums in issue"*.

Benefits of allocation to the SCT

The court will be able to deal with the claim much more swiftly and will be able to allocate to it a more proportionate amount of time. The result is that neither party will expend inordinate amounts of time on legal preparation and the saving in costs will be substantial. The normal rules of evidence do not apply in the SCT, but it is still important to prepare witness statements with exhibits properly.

In the SCT it is even possible that the court can be persuaded to deal with the claim on paper, without a hearing, if both parties agree. That might be an attractive option if a tenant's solicitors are worried that they will not recover their costs. But normally there is a conflict of evidence on the question of notice and the court will need to make a decision whether the tenant is telling the truth when they say they reported the disrepair many times.

Costs after trial in the SCT

Even if a claimant tenant succeeds on a small part of their claim, the damages are likely to be modest and the court will only order the fixed costs appropriate to the SCT. Effectively this limits the total costs claim to less than £1,000.

There are downsides to trial in the SCT – in any claim where the landlord succeeds in defeating its entirely, costs are not ordinarily recoverable. However, it is possible to argue that the claimant should pay the defendant's costs, even in the SCT. Of particular relevance is whether the claimant has behaved unreasonably or dishonestly, or has sought to exaggerate their claim. I will leave it to practitioners to recognise when it may be appropriate to make the application. The law on how to do it is in the White Book.

Chapter summary/key takeaways

- Although claims are nearly always issued in a distant County Court hearing centre, they should be transferred immediately to the landlord's home court if possible.

- Careful consideration should be given to the issue of allocation and the claimant's assertion that the case should be listed in the Fast Track should not necessarily be accepted.

- Few landlords' representatives recognise the availability of this simple but necessary exercise in the assessment of a claim and the subsequent procedural steps or application necessary to address the serious issue caused by allocation to the Fast Track.

- A landlord needs to be confident of its stance on getting repairs done quickly-tenants should not be allowed to delay them. Landlords should ask for an injunction against the tenant for any persistent refusal of access.

- Landlords have a duty to carry out repairs as swiftly as possible following notice received through a Letter of Claim. They cannot be criticised for as soon as possible.

- The Court should not allocate a disrepair claim to the fast track if the circumstances do not justify such allocation.

- Where the claimant cannot honestly ask for an injunction for specific performance, and the damages claimed are less than £10,000, or both the cost of the works and the claim for damages are less than £1,000, the claim should not proceed on the FT and will be allocated to the SCT.

In the next chapter, we will look at disclosure and inspection, which is more relevant to FT trials, as the SCT does not require the parties to carry out the formal disclosure process.

CHAPTER NINETEEN

DISCLOSURE AND INSPECTION

In the Fast Track and the Multi-Track the process of Disclosure will take place in every case. It is governed by CPR 31, which you should read, along with the notes in the White Book.

Once a claim is underway, assuming that disclosure, or at least full disclosure has not been given at the Protocol stage (because you have successfully objected to pre-action disclosure) you will need to engage in disclosure within the trial process.

CPR 31 addresses disclosure and inspection and this is not intended to be a definitive guide to the process. Again, if you are litigating these claims, it is important to understand your general disclosure rights and duties. This means knowing what documents you are entitled to insist upon seeing and what documents you have to be certain that you have disclosed.

This is because the obligation to disclose is backed up by a binding confirmation that the party has complied with their obligations. CPR 21.23 says that *"proceedings for contempt of court may be brought against person if he makes, or causes to be made, a false disclosure statement, without an honest belief in its truth."*

Putting it bluntly, if you knowingly hide the existence of documents, you can go to prison, as can your opponent's solicitor, or the claimant themselves.

This chapter considers disclosure only with regard to particular issues in disrepair claims.

Directions and disclosure in the SCT

The court will also fix a date for the hearing when it sends out the Directions. That should be within weeks and not months (as is normal for the FT).

There are some 'standard directions' available for certain types of disputes, and these can be adapted to suit housing disrepair claims.

In the SCT there is no formal procedure for disclosure – CPR 27.2 (1) (b) expressly says so, but the parties must disclose documents on which they intend to rely and which may be helpful to their opponent.

The court will send the parties a directions questionnaire to allow it to give directions for the hearing, which will include an order that the parties file and serve copies of all documents on which they intend to rely at the hearing no later than 14 days before it is listed.

Disclosure in the FT and the MT is more complex.

Meaning of 'Disclosure' in the FT and the MT

CPR 31.2 says that the meaning of the word is limited to a statement that a document exists or has existed. That means you do not necessarily have to produce the document for disclosure, in fact you may not even be able to do so-you have to say whether it is or has been in your control.

This can have particular relevance when a landlord's document retention policy results in the destruction of historical repairs records earlier than prudent. It is necessary to state in the disclosure process if you no longer hold records because they have been destroyed.

Equally, if as a defendant you ask the claimant to disclose certain documents, they must sign their disclosure statement confirming that they had the document in their possession but it has been destroyed or lost etc.

'Possession or control'

The obligation to disclose the existence of documents does not relate only to those in your physical possession. It also covers documents which are in the 'control' of a party – see CPR 31.8.

This includes records held by others which can be obtained by application or request from them. The party only has to have a right to possession, or a right to inspect or take a copy of a document to make it disclosable.

Meaning of "document"

This word does not only mean paper documents. It also applies to anything in which information of any description is recorded. That includes computer files, email records, audio recordings and photographs/videos. It will also include mobile and landline call records where relevant. See CPR 31.4.

Therefore, landlords need to think carefully about what 'documents' tenants can be asked to disclose. For instance, it is important to ask claimant tenants for their phone records if they are alleging that they gave notice by telephone. Additionally, if they allege that the property is too cold because of disrepair, their heating bills are relevant. Further, if they say they have been caused any ill-health or injury, their medical records are disclosable for the whole period over which the injury is said to have occurred.

'Standard' disclosure

The extent of disclosure necessary is mandated by the track on which the claim is allocated.

In SCT claims there is no such thing as disclosure per se and the parties only have to comply with the limited obligation to provide copies of documents on which they rely and which might harm their case etc.

in FT claims, the parties are ordered by the court to give standard disclosure (under CPR 31.10) and the court may even dispense with or limit that process (by CPR 31.5 (1) (b)). Also, the parties may agree in writing between themselves to dispense with or limit standard disclosure.

In compiling the list, although documents have to be identified in a "convenient order and manner and as concisely as possible", it is possible to list classes of documents by date brackets-e.g. "Emails between claimant and defendant from [date] to [date]." Many people spend hours listing every single individual document, which is unnecessary.

In MT claims, the parties must follow the rather complicated timetable in CPR 31.5 (3) unless the court orders otherwise.

Disclosure relates to all 'relevant' documents

When giving standard disclosure you must disclose documents on which you rely, which adversely affect your own case or that of another party or which support any other party's case (CPR 31.6).

This is a very important principle – it is not permissible to hold back a document from disclosure because it might damage one's case. It is important to recognise that obligation and to check with the repairs team that there is nothing waiting to be discovered by people looking at other documents. Litigants, both claimant and defendant, have to remember that their credibility and reputation is at stake in each case.

Disclosure by landlords in the FT

So far as a landlord is concerned, if disclosure has been provided within the Pre-Action Protocol there will be little left to disclose, but a check still needs to be made that no documents have been missed out.

Sources of documentary records will include the various repairs team software databases, both reactive and long-term maintenance and improvement systems, the tenancy file and records of any complaints. There may well be email trails which are relevant to the carrying out of works and which explain decisions to proceed with or cancel various jobs.

Disclosure by tenants in the FT

In theory a tenant ought also to have disclosed relevant documents in the operation of the Protocol. In practice they rarely do so and it is often necessary to ask for documents on which the landlord would wish to rely.

In the FT the court can order less than standard disclosure – see CPR 28, PD para 3.6(1) (c) and (4), but in disrepair cases this may not be a sensible course of action as the landlord needs to ensure that the tenant discloses all necessary documents.

There will be circumstances in which a tenant has possession or control of documents which are likely to assist the landlord in the defence of the claim. The most obvious of those (as mentioned above) are:

- telephone records when they say they have repeatedly called the landlord;

- medical records in cases where the tenant says they have suffered stress or ill-health. Reports are only privileged when prepared for the purpose of litigation;

- utility bills where they say that they have heated and ventilated a property adequately but it is still too cold;

- emails or texts which mention the state of repair of the property, whether to the landlord or to others.

Inspection

Once a document is disclosed, the other side has a right to inspect it unless:

- it is no longer in the control (not just possession) of the party disclosing it;

- the party has a right or duty to withhold inspection (most likely because it is privileged);

- the party considers that it would be disproportionate to the issues in the case to permit a category or class of documents, in which case inspection is not required and statement must be made to that effect;

- it is "closed material" under CPR 79-highly unlikely in a disrepair claim!

Duty of disclosure continues throughout the proceedings

Until judgement is given and an order made, the parties must remember their continuing duty to the court to disclose the existence of any document coming to that parties notice for the first time after disclosure has taken place.

This is particularly relevant where works are being carried out on a property as a case proceeds. It is crucial that those documents created during the works are disclosed to the other side. Another class of documents likely to be created during the proceedings is the data logging monitoring records. Landlords will need to obtain and analyse records created by remote or in situ property monitoring equipment.

Equally, it applies to a tenant who receives something as small as a card which informs them that the landlord called to carry out works but they were not available to give access. The same goes for updated medical records, continuing utility bills etc. useful evidence may be obtained from a tenant when works are carried out, for instance if they make no difference to the quantum of the utility bills.

Applications for specific disclosure

If a tenant's solicitor refuses to disclose the relevant documents, it will be necessary to make an application for specific disclosure pursuant to CPR 31.12. A party can ask for disclosure of documents or classes of documents (particularly anything named in or inferred to exist by the POC) and further documents which must exist as appears either from the face of a list or in the list itself.

The court has to consider the reasonableness of any search expected of the respondent. The applicant needs to give evidence why they are not satisfied with the disclosure afforded thus far by the respondent and why they anticipate that the specific disclosure sought would be proportionate and relevant to and probative of the issues.

Timing of applications for specific disclosure

Such applications should be dealt with at the same time as other case management decisions if possible, to keep costs down, i.e. they should not be listed separately. This is particularly important because the court may consider that it is appropriate to reserve the question of costs to await determination of the question whether the documents disclosed have been probative and relevant.

Additionally, if an order for a further search is made but that search proves fruitless or the documents found in disclosed prove to be irrelevant, the applicant may be penalised in costs.

Disclosure can only be ordered in respect of matters which are expressly pleaded, so it is important to say in the Defence why particular facts are relevant if an application is contemplated.

An order for specific disclosure can include a requirement that the respondent carries out a search for any documents which are disclosable.

Documents mentioned in a statement of case

Such documents should be disclosed as a matter of course and are often attached as an appendix or schedule to the pleading.

If a party fails to disclose a document which has been mentioned in pleadings, a witness statement or summary, an affidavit or an expert's report, an application can be made under CPR 31.14 for disclosure and inspection of that document. Any documents which are privileged remain protected and cannot be inspected, unless it could be argued that privilege has been waived.

If a document is not specifically mentioned but its existence has to be inferred, an application needs to be made under CPR 31.12.

Some tenant surveyors do not include a copy of their instructions in their report and it is wise to request one, although only the substance of instructions need be disclosed.

Chapter summary/key takeaways

- Disclosure should be used as an opportunity to reassess the strength of the claim against the landlord and to ensure that the witness statements can deal with all the issues of fact which are likely to arise.

- Social landlords often have sophisticated repairs software, which will need to be interrogated to provide proper disclosure. It is sometimes a challenge to be confident that this has been done successfully by the repairs team, who are often overworked.

In the next chapter we will look at drafting witness statements for disrepair trials.

CHAPTER TWENTY

WITNESS STATEMENTS

Some of the preparation necessary for trial will already have been undertaken in the earlier skirmishes concerning summary judgement, striking out the claim and allocation to track. Those witness statements can either be used in the trial or fresh statements will need to be drafted.

Witness statements in disrepair claims will be necessary primarily in two circumstances: first, where the progress of the legal proceedings has been such that issues have arisen which need to be determined by the judge (rare) and second, where the surveyor in their report does not address the factual history of the tenancy, to the extent it is relevant.

Basic requirements of witness statements

It is surprising how many lawyers seem to be unaware of the need to follow the CPR. Anyone preparing a trial should read the requirements as to the format of witness statements, which can be found in CPR 32.8 and PD 32.19.

For instance, the statement should be "fully legible" and "should normally be typed on one side of the paper only. Page numbers should be inserted and paragraphs should be numbered. All numbers, including dates should be expressed in figures rather than words. If any document is referred to, the reference to it should be included either in the margin, or in bold text in the body of the statement.

Exhibits must be clearly labelled with the exhibit number and paginated separately to the witness statement.

Witnesses must prepare their statement in their own language if they do not speak English. They must then be translated by a certified translator.

Witness statements drafted for pre-trial applications

Occasionally there are issues which need to be addressed by the trial judge before the hearing. These can be last-minute disputes about the extent of disclosure, or the timing of service of witness statements. If the question concerns disclosure, it should have been dealt with long before, but the parties sometimes find themselves close to the hearing with outstanding arguments as to what should be disclosed.

Sometimes those arguments are so important that, for instance, they can lead to making a last-minute application for specific disclosure which ends up being listed before the trial judge. Such circumstances are thankfully rare and will cause significant wasted costs, which might be visited upon the party at fault. Occasionally, there are documents in the possession of one party or the other which can be obtained swiftly and produced, even on the day of trial.

Alternatively, one party or the other may serve their witness statements late. Arguments about service of statements are usually arid and pointless in most cases, despite what is said in *Mitchell* and the subsequent case law. If a party is not prejudiced the opponent by late service of witness statements, it is normally pointless to object to their admission. The attitude of most District Judges is that the parties should be encouraged to resolve the dispute on its merits, particularly if the trial is listed and would not take place if statements are not admitted.

However, there are some circumstances in which a judge might be inclined to refuse to admit witness statements and at this stage it need only be said that the question of trial preparation can throw up serious procedural issues which need to be addressed by the trial judge before the commencement of the evidence.

Any witness statement in support of arguments on legal issues will need to exhibit the chain of correspondence between the parties. If the facts relied on our clear from the correspondence, then the witness statement should not go into great depth about how and issue developed. The statement should just say that the correspondence is self-explanatory.

Witnesses as to the history of the tenancy

Although a good part of the dispute in a disrepair claim concerns the history of the condition of the property, in many cases the Housing Officer or other employees of the landlord will know facts on which the landlord will want to rely.

For instance, where a tenant has made no reports of defects yet the property is in a very poor state, it is necessary to investigate the reason for that situation. The tenant may have been living elsewhere, they may have been cultivating or selling drugs, or had other reasons why they did not want the landlord to attend at the property.

The evidence as to the history of the tenancy is unlikely to be found only on the repairs file. There may be material in the tenancy file which throw light on the situation. Often the tenancy application form will provide relevant material on the occupants.

The personal knowledge of the Housing Officer and others can expand upon those documents and notes. A detailed witness statement needs to be prepared, exhibiting the relevant diary entries and documents, explaining the landlord's point of view regarding the repairs history.

The witness statement should contain a reasoned chronological narrative, setting out the basic facts on which the landlord relies and referring to the documents for more detailed content. Brevity is desirable, because in a short trial (lasting only half a day or a day) the District Judge will not have time to read dozens of pages of history.

They will need to be told the basic facts and to be taken to the documentary exhibits which support the landlord's case.

The witness statement should refer to the exhibit by page number so any reference is easy to follow.

Chapter summary/key takeaways

- The preparation of clear and informative witness statements is an essential skill. Because witnesses do not give evidence in chief, the judge needs to know the essential facts from the witness statement alone.

- You cannot rely on material beneficial to the landlord coming out in cross-examination. If there is a gap in the evidence, tenants will take advantage of it and the only weight to prevent that is to anticipate it.

- Getting the format and content of witness statements right will help the judge understand the facts and make it easier for the trial to be dealt with swiftly.

In the next chapter we will look briefly at the conduct of disrepair trials.

PART V

PREPARING FOR TRIAL

If the claim has continued despite your best efforts to refer it to alternative dispute resolution and to reduce the areas of dispute, you will need to prepare for trial. It is not possible in a book of this nature to give detailed instructions on how to prepare for a trial in general.

It is fair to say that you are likely to need lawyers, or at least a direct access barrister to help you from the outset. This is particularly true in getting ready to undertake a contested trial. I will therefore say a little about the particular features of preparing for disrepair claims which might be of help to those preparing for and attending trial.

CHAPTER TWENTY-ONE

THE TRIAL

Disrepair claims are usually listed before District Judges or, these days, Deputy District Judges. Occasionally they may be listed before County Court Judges or Recorders. This is not ideal, because any appeal from the latter will be more expensive and time-consuming.

It would not be possible in this book to address the conduct of a trial in any detail. Below I have included some features which may help in preparing the case to go to an advocate. That individual will know what to do in a trial, although I have made observations about peculiarities of disrepair trials.

Provision in the directions for a view of the property

In some cases, a landlord might want the Judge hearing the trial to see the property for themselves.

This is particularly so where a tenant is being difficult about the quality of works carried out but objectively, they are difficult to criticise. Alternatively, where the tenant's lifestyle is such that the landlord wants the court to make a judgement on the effect of any disrepair as against the loss of amenity caused by the tenant's own acts of waste.

If there is a hearing fixed before the trial to consider preparations, an application might be made for a view to take place. There is likely to be judicial reluctance unless good grounds can be proved. It helps if the property is very close to the court. These days, with the closure of so many county courts, that is often difficult to arrange. Further, judges are routinely given to much work and may not have time to fit in a view.

A view can be organised, if the court is willing, to start early in the morning on the day of trial, e.g. by 9:30 AM, and the judge can meet the parties at the building so that the trial can proceed as close to 10:30 AM as possible.

As an alternative to a view, the landlord might wish to attend and take multiple photographs or produce a video showing the property, concentrating on issues which the landlord wishes to emphasise to the court.

Ensuring that the judge is able to deal expeditiously with the hearing

Landlords need to be prepared to make up for failings on the part of claimant solicitors in trial preparation. Even if a reminder of the need for compliance is sent, it is common to receive a trial bundle which fails to comply with the Guidelines in one or more respects.

A Judge hearing a disrepair claim will sometimes have to get through 500-700 pages of trial bundle, a significant part of which will be relevant to the issues. They need every assistance they can be offered. They are unlikely to have been given any reading time by their listing staff and, if the trial is due to start a 10 AM and they arrive at court at 9 AM, they will have very limited time in which to consider the bundle. If that bundle is difficult to navigate, the judge is likely to begin the trial understandably annoyed.

As a result, it is sometimes necessary to prepare a trial bundle which does comply with the Guidelines, so that the hearing can go ahead without the judge being inconvenienced from the outset.

Trial bundles

In the lead up to the trial it will be necessary to agree the content of a bundle with the other side, and for one or other party to create a PDF and possibly a paper version of that bundle.

Often, claimant solicitors do not appreciate the need to include certain documents in the trial bundle. This is particularly so if the evidence given in interim applications is still relevant to points in dispute at the trial. For instance, what a claimant tenant said in response to an application for further information or for specific disclosure may merit cross-examination at trial.

PDF bundles

It is essential that litigators are familiar with the "General Guidance on PDF Bundles" issued by the judiciary for the assistance of practitioners submitting them[31].

Briefly, they must:

- be the subject of optical character recognition, so that the document becomes word-searchable and words can be highlighted

- all documents should appear in portrait mode, but if the original is a landscape version then it should be inserted so it can be read with a 90° rotation clockwise.

- The default view should be 100%

- if a core bundle is needed then it should be produced complying with the same requirements as a paper bundle

- the number of PDF bundles should be limited so that the judge does not need to have a significant number of PDF files open during the hearing. If it is essential to separate documents, it should be done by document type rather than file size.

- bundles of particular types of document should generally be chronological if possible

- all pages must be numbered, if possible using computer-generated numbering, or at least typing the numbers. Hand numbering is not permitted. If the bundle is split into sections then the page number should be preceded by the section identifying character, e.g. "B 17".

---

[31] available at:Available at : https://www.judiciary.uk/wp-content/uploads/2020/05/GENERAL-GUIDANCE-ON-PDF-BUNDLES-f-1.pdf

- pagination must not mask relevant details on the original document

- scans should be of 300 dpi or less to avoid slow strolling or rendering all significant documents and all sections in bundles must be bookmarked for ease of navigation, with an appropriate description as the bookmark, together with the page number of the document

- an index or table of contents should be prepared and if practicable each line should be hyperlinked to the individual document

- all PDF files must contain a short version of the name of the case, the bundle number and the hearing date, e.g. "Smith v Anytown Housing Association Ltd, bundle B, 1 July 2022"

- if adding supplementary bundle after the file has been transmitted to a judge, the party must check whether the additional material is to be added to the original or submitted as a separate file. But in any case, pages should be sequentially numbered. If pages are to be added within a bundle, they should be sub- numbered (e.g. 123.1, 123.2 etc)

- e-bundles must be less than 36 MB in aggregate if sent to the justice.gov eddress. The ejudiciary.net website will accept bundles of 150 MB in aggregate. Some courts will accept links to file uploads, e.g. Google Drive, OneDrive or similar.

- emails with a bundle attached for a remote hearing must contain in the subject line the case number, case name, hearing date, name of the judge and, in capitals "REMOTE HEARING".

Remote hearings

It is possible to undertake a disrepair trial remotely. Some claimants have a poor Internet connection and it is therefore difficult to see them clearly. This works to their advantage if there is any suggestion that they are not being truthful, as the judge will find it more difficult to see facial expressions and therefore to detect discomfort or nervousness.

Additionally, although views are rare in any event, is obviously not possible to organise one for a remote hearing.

Skeleton arguments

Many District Judges are not landlord and tenant lawyers and they are likely to need assistance with the background law relating to disrepair claims. This means providing a skeleton argument which addresses when liability will arise, how the court should approach the question of notice, whether there is an issue as to mitigation loss etc.

Further, in cases where the history of repairs to any particular defect is anything other than simple, it will be necessary to set out the page numbers of the relevant documents, so that the Judge can follow the history of each defect as evidenced by records, rather than as set out in the claimant's witness statement, which is unlikely to reflect the records.

It will also be necessary to deal with the expert evidence in the skeleton argument, which by the date of trial should be agreed. The claimant's surveyor is unlikely to have addressed the central issue of section 11 (3) or the history of repairs.

Scott schedules

The surveyors will usually have had some contact, although this should not be necessary if the landlord's surveyor has been efficient and has ordered the necessary works.

The court will expect the parties to prepare a Scott Schedule of the allegations, admissions costings and comments by each party.

Attendance by surveyors

Often the condition of the property on the day the surveyor inspected is not in dispute and it will be unnecessary to call the surveyors. This is a point which needs to be made both in the Defence and stressed in the skeleton argument. If there is no dispute between the parties as to the condition of the property and the works which need to be done, the value of the claim is commensurately lower.

The works as recommended by the tenant's surveyor will not ordinarily be central. This is because of the principle that the nature and extent of remedial works is a matter for the landlord, provided that they act reasonably. If a tenant believes that the landlord's surveyor has not specified adequate works, unless the specification is clearly and obviously wrong, the tenant's remedy lies in damages rather than an order that particular works should be carried out.

Therefore, even if there is some dispute as to method between the surveyors, it should be possible to avoid calling surveyors to give evidence at trial. This can be addressed in the Defence and repeated in the skeleton argument.

Procedure in the trial

Whether in the SCT or the FT, the trial follows the same format. The claimant tenant will give evidence first. They should not need to give any supplementary evidence once they are in the witness box but, for instance, works may have been carried out between the signing of the witness statement and the trial and the tenant will want to talk about them.

It is important to anticipate that possibility and to obtain good, up-to-date evidence about the condition of the property, including confirmation that the tenant is happy with the current state of repair of the property.

Cross-examination

Cross-examination of a tenant will address issues such as how the tenant came to instruct solicitors, whether they did give notice as alleged in the claimant's pleadings and evidence, which defects they noticed themselves and which were pointed out by the claims prospector or the surveyor, the effect of defects, the reasons for tenant damage etc.

The landlord's surveyor (who will often be giving evidence of fact as well as opinion) and lay witness(es) will be cross-examined on methods of giving notice, repairs targets, specific delays in repairs, repair methods etc.

Closing speeches and judgement

After the parties have called their evidence, the parties give their closing speeches, the defendant goes first and the claimant has the last word. The defendant has the right to reply to mistakes of law on the part of the claimant, or to errors of fact.

Judgement in disrepair claims is often reserved, because the issues can be factually complex and time is short in a trial listed for one day or even less.

Costs to be paid by the claimant

Assuming that the defendant landlord is successful, the claim will be dismissed and the tenant will be ordered to pay the costs.

Costs in the SCT:

In the SCT, the parties can usually only recover limited costs, being the costs of issue, the court costs for starting the claim and the hearing fee on the SCT basis, and the surveyor's fees, which are limited to £750. Those limits can be overridden if the landlord can show that the claimant has behaved unreasonably.

Costs in the FT:

if the claim has remained in the FT, either because the landlord has decided that they want to be able to recover their costs, or because they were unsuccessful in asking for allocation to the SCT, more substantial costs can be recovered by either party.

These days almost every tenant has legal expenses insurance and this should not be an issue. The court will ask for the defendant's N 260 and costs will be summarily assessed. The court will usually order that those costs are payable within 14 or 21 days, as the money has to be obtained from the insurers.

It is not uncommon for a landlord to spend between £15,000 and £30,000 defending a disrepair claim. After assessment, they are likely to recover a substantial part of that, providing they can show that the claimant put them to the trouble and expense of collecting the relevant evidence.

Generally, the question of proportionality trumps all when it comes to costs in disrepair claims. It is the value at which the tenant's claim was put which is relevant to the question of proportionality in assessing costs which a claimant should pay. Additionally if a claimant's conduct has unnecessarily increased the costs, whether by their being obstructive or failing to particularise their claim properly, the court will be more willing to reimburse the landlord's costs to a greater extent.

Damages in disrepair claims

In theory, landlords should not lose disrepair claims, because they will have spotted any cases in which there has been a genuine failure to repair and will have made offers to settle.

But some trials don't go so well; e.g. a claimant is believed despite the complete lack of corroboration of the alleged complaints, the landlord surveyor misses something in the records, or the claimant does not accept an offer (very rare).

Damages can be awarded on a variety of methods of calculation. I have already mentioned that the court can choose from the available cases, but most judges will rely on the method used in *Wallace v Manchester CC*, which gives a broad ranging tariff, which runs from a few hundred pounds a year to a few thousand.

As I have said, the method of calculation is addressed in Dowding & Reynolds on Dilapidations and Luba et al on Housing Conditions. Hopefully it will be rare that you need to refer to it. In 25 years I have only had to do so on a couple of occasions, so it is not worth spending significant time on the issue in this book, because we are concerned with defeating the claim rather than compromising or losing it.

Costs to be paid by the defendant

If the worst has happened, the claimant rarely ends up the true winner even in the Fast Track, because the costs incurred by tenant solicitors are so disproportionate to the amount of damages at stake that they are usually summarily assessed to a modest proportion of the original claim.

Tenant solicitors seem to generate very substantial fees without much to show for them. For this reason, when presented with an N260, it is worth getting a costs draughtsman to analyse it before the trial. But in any event, many items of work will be obviously open to challenge and proportionality is likely to be of even greater importance.

Chapter summary/key takeaways

- We have briefly looked at the conduct of disrepair trials, to the extent they differ from other County Court claims. There is plenty more that can be said about the conduct of the trial, probably another book's worth of work.

- Even if a claimant is successful at trial, they frequently do not recover significant costs from the landlord, because awards of damages are very much lower than those originally claimed and specific performance is rarely ordered.

- As this is primarily aimed at people who are involved in the preparation and pre-trial stages of the claim, and it is already quite long enough, I am going to refrain from going into further detail!

We have reached the end of the journey to trial and I hope the book has been useful!

EPILOGUE / CONCLUSION

If you have got this far, you deserve a medal! I hope you will have taken on board the message. Unless you are working in an organisation which does not care about its tenants, most disrepair claims are likely to be unjustified. With the material in this book, you should be able to begin to fight back against unjustified claims, or at least to know when to settle.

Please do tell me if you find any mistakes, of any sort.

APPENDIX ONE

EXAMPLE STAGE 3 COMPLAINTS FINDING

DRAFT STAGE 3 LETTER FROM CHIEF EXECUTIVE IN RESPONSE TO COMPLAINT BY MS ADELE SMITH

DECISION LETTER AND OFFER OF COMPENSATION

Dear Ms Smith

I write to you direct, rather than your Solicitor because the Council's Complaints Process is designed to work outside the legal system and without you needing a lawyer. In fact, you already set out your complaints very clearly in the list you wrote on 15 March 2021. I have used that as the basis of my investigations and I have looked at the history of your tenancy with that in mind.

It has been a time-consuming job to go back over the history of repairs and to understand what has happened. My apologies for the very slow reply to your complaint, because you should have heard from me some months ago. I know that the Council Solicitors had their own issues and, as a result, it hasn't been considered nearly as swiftly as I would like. I will deal with that at the end of this decision letter. I'm going to suggest that your rent arrears are reduced by an amount I will work out and tell you at the end of the letter.

The letter is very long because I wanted to set out for you the whole of the history of your tenancy, so you can see how things have developed and the reasons for my conclusions. Like any of these properties in Amherst Village, they do need a lot of work to keep up to a reasonable standard and yours is no exception. The properties have timber windows rather than UPVC, which are difficult to keep in perfect condition. It's also true that condensation causes problems in old buildings like these, and I cannot offer you compensation just because you have experienced condensation problems. Your repairs history shows 77 repairs over 20 years, averaging at 3.85 repairs per year, a normal amount for such properties. The Council has 15,000 properties and carries out 54,000 repairs a year.

Your complaint lists the following issues you have raised with the Council:

1) *I was with no heating for 2 years and promised Central Heating by January 2020.*

2) *When electrical surveyor came in January he told me electric for heater is not connected to economy 7, therefore I have been paying the most expensive form of electricity since 2010.*

3) *The Council hasn't been touch to change this.*

4) *The electrician that installed the heating system advised me not to turn the heaters on so I am still with no adequate heating.*

5) *The windows have been unfinished for more than a year.*

6) *The repair/appointment team is useless, and I have a text in January 2021 telling me they were coming in December 2020!!!*

7) *We have been to Court 4 times and Anytown Borough Council keeps wasting the tax payers money by delaying the process in which I get to put to shame the repairs team and management by going to a proper hearing.*

8) *I want the arrears cleared and to be moved to a cottage in the Amherst Village with Central Heating and patio and shed.*

9) *If I get that I will have no need to pursue my complaints anymore.*

10) *I have hundreds of emails back and forward from/to the Council that proves I am right so I don't want to meet with your Solicitor unless you offer the above terms.*

I will look at each of these later, but so that you know how I'm thinking, I will try to give you what I hope is a fair summary of the history of your tenancy as I see it.

The history of your tenancy

1. You applied for housing as you were 'homeless and in priority need' in your flat was given to you on the basis of a licence which the Council gave you as temporary accommodation. When you originally applied for housing you said you wanted to live in Anytown centre because you intended to study and understandably could not afford a car to get to college. You were given accommodation as you were in priority need under the Homeless Persons part of the Housing Act 1985. Your tenancy began as a licence about 22 years ago. You moved in on 30 January 1999. Originally it was a "temporary tenancy" and was converted into a secure tenancy on 6 January 2000. You were about 24 years old when you took the flat on, so you have now spent about half your life there. You had two children, and the children effectively grew up there.

2. You made a transfer application, which was received on 24 June 2017. At that point you said you would only live in the Old Town in a house. As you know accommodation has not been available to allow you to transfer into such a property.

3. You fell into arrears of rent and they were £180.70 by March 2020 There is lots of correspondence about rent arrears over the rest of your tenancy. A claim for possession was first issued on 21 June 2020.

4. It's obvious that you were not happy with the flat, because you made another application for transfer/mutual exchange on 3 February 2014, in which you said that you wanted to move for health reasons and poor housing conditions. You complained that the property was unsuitable. You were and remain (as I understand it) severely affected by an accident and there are minor adaptations to the property. You said "*I want a cottage, because I don't want to move out of the area but I'm fed up with this end of the village and need a garden (to store wheelchairs bikes and sit outside with my children) I want central heating because my house is too cold and expensive to heat and I think the cottages and houses in the village have central heating.*" You only wished to be transferred to somewhere in central Anytown.

5. Another notice seeking possession was issued on 17 February 2016 and an order for possession was made on 6 September 2018 for £613.97 arrears, suspended on the basis you pay your arrears. A new notice seeking possession was served on 12 February 2020 and another one on 14 April 2021. The Tenancy Sustainment Officer had been involved with you and were clearly struggling to make ends meet with your then approximately 18 and 16 year old sons.

6. In 2019 Your son was causing serious problems in the area. In April 2019 he was arrested for supplying cannabis to an undercover police Officer. The flat was searched and 610 g of cannabis leaf was found, which he admitted was his in interview. On 26 April 2019 the Council had to write to you, warning you that your tenancy was at risk and pointing out that you are responsible for your son's behaviour. Later he pleaded guilty to 2 counts of possession of cannabis and was given a suspended sentence. On 6 June 2020 your son admitted two counts of supplying heroin and was sent to prison. I mention this because it's part of the overall picture of the issues that you have been experiencing and that the Council has had to deal with as part of the tenancy.

7. I see that your flat was logged on the Amherst Village external planned works programme in October 2019 and put on the gas central heating programme in January 2020. I know that one of your major complaints is that you have not received gas central heating. I think you've subsequently been told that it proved impossible put it in.

8. On 24 January 2020 you complained to your Housing Officer in an email about "Rubbish etc". However I want to look at that because you were also complaining about repairs not being done. In summary you said:

    8.1. your house was so neglected that it was making you feel depressed and you are going to your doctor for help;

    8.2. You were spending 'a fortune' on electricity to heat it because the heaters were wasteful and inefficient;

8.3. the blinds moved because of the draught coming through the windows and the walls around the windows let draughts in;

8.4. you complained about that contractors trying to fix the problems had "totally destroyed" the frames and original window furniture but had done a poor job of it. They had changed the fixed frame in the kitchen into an opening window, which you felt was ill-advised;

8.5. the bathroom floor had been dangerously loose for more than a year and the contractors who were supposed to fix it did not call when they were supposed to, so nothing happened for months until someone came and put silicon around the bath tub even though the whole thing was supposed to be changed;

8.6. central heating been promised by 2020 but had not happened (see above);

8.7. you had a number of complaints about conditions outside the flat, but we aren't concerned with those here, so I won't list them. At that time, the real nub of your complaint was: inefficient heaters and no central heating, draughty and badly repaired windows, dangerously loose bathroom floor.

9. Originally you got a reply from Flora Withers, the Lead Neighbourhood Housing Officer, dated 26 February 2020, saying that the repairs department would reply and apologising for your problems. She also explained what was being done in relation to the issues you had outside the flat.

10. You also got a reply from Brent Rogers about the central heating that you were not happy with and you complained again by email on 14 June 2020.

11. Eric Barton wrote to you in answer to your complaints on 18 August 2020 (see below) giving you the option of asking for the matter to be referred to the Chief Executive, but you did not take up that offer. Instead it looks as if you waited until the matter came back to court on 28 November 2016, when you complained that repairs had not been done properly or on time and made a counterclaim. It is

217

unfortunate that you did not come to me at that time, because I am sure that this would have avoided the need for all the subsequent unpleasantness of the court proceedings. Also your arrears have built up significantly in the meantime.

12. That handwritten claim is what I reproduced above as the basis of your complaint as it stood when you went to court. I am told that when you were at court you confirmed that there were no outstanding works needed at that time you were happy with the state of the flat, although I see from the repairs records that there was a lot of correspondence between you and the repairs department around and after that time, which I will try to summarise below if it's relevant.

13. While going through your records, I found a letter dated 24 May 2021 from you. You gave an address of "40 Dunroving Road, Anytown." I could not find any reply from you explaining why you weren't living at your flat, but I assume that you have moved back in by now.

14. I've seen the table that you provided us with and it does provide details of complaints made by you between 3 April 2020 and 6 May 2020. I will try to summarise what you are saying and what has been extracted from the records in relation to each complaint:

The windows

14.1.   You complained that the house was "neglected" so that the windows let in water and wind, that complaint being made on 24 January, 4 February, 13 April, 6 May and 11 May 2020, and you said the works were finished in early 2021. I think you know that the Council does its very best with houses in Amherst Village, but because they are listed/in a Conservation Area, it's very difficult to bring them up to modern day standards, and the Council has got to bear this in mind when repairing properties. This is particularly so with these windows. They are difficult to draught proof and double glazed and as a result you've always complained that they let in cold and cost you extra money. This is an unfortunate side-effect of the type of windows you have.

14.1.1. The Council records say that the windows had been on a planned external maintenance programme. Whenever large-scale works are planned there is inevitably a delay for some occupiers, and they may have to put up with a less than perfect situation given the difficulty of organising works for so many properties.

14.1.2. There is a record of a callout to attend to board up the kitchen window on 20 January 2020. On 27 January the job was appointed for 29 January to overhaul the window including the kitchen but you missed the appointment and the job was closed. I do not know whether the job which was raised on 27 January 2020 to repair the new windows applied to windows other than the kitchen.

14.1.3. The planned maintenance manager apparently checked that the windows had been repaired and painted on programme on 3 February 2020, although this seems to be at odds with her assertion that they were still letting in rain on 13 April 2020, when the kitchen window was still boarded up. The way I read the records, it is similar to what was happening with the bathroom floor and you and the Council were finding it difficult to coordinate a time when some works could be done;

14.1.4. they were eventually fixed to your satisfaction in March 2021. As a result, I believe that although it's arguable whether the Council was falling short in its duty to repair your windows, as opposed to them being of a similar standard to others in the area, I am prepared to find that you should be entitled to some compensation for the time between when you reported and when I think they should have been draught proofed and repaired temporarily, three months after you complained. I'm prepared to offer you £1,000 in compensation for this part of your complaint. I do not think that the Council should offer you any significant amount of money for the cost of heating because these windows were only single glazed and they were not very efficient, but all similar properties in the area suffered from the same problem.

The central heating

14.2.   you were told in a mailshot that gas central heating would be installed in a programme in 2020 but you correctly complained by email on 9 February 2021 that it had not been installed.

14.2.1. The records seem to indicate that there had been no reports from you that the storage heating system was not working.

14.2.2. I see that the contractor from Gerbert Electrical who did the upgrade noticed that you were using portable panel heaters to heat the rooms. You told the electrical contractor that you did not turn the heating on as you had been using your own panel heating, presumably because the installed system was too expensive to run. He told you to contact your supplier to get this sorted out, which you did while he was there. He did not tell you not to switch them on, but that you might be charged at a higher rate because of the problem he had found.

14.2.3. It transpired that it was not possible to fit gas central heating because there was no gas supply and new electric heating was installed on 13 February 2021.

14.2.4. You have subsequently said that you been told that the Economy 7 meter was wrongly configured, so you were paying for more expensive electricity than you needed. The Council is not entitled to interfere with the electricity meter and that is something that the supplier should have fixed.

14.2.5. I recognise that the storage heating system would have been expensive to run, whether as a result of the problem with the meter or because they are inefficient. However it was not out of repair as far as I can tell from the records.

14.2.6. Again, communication with you could have been much better and I believe that you should be entitled to some compensation to reflect the difficulties you had in sorting things out. I'm prepared to offer you a total sum of £500 to reflect this, although again I'm not convinced that the problem was that repairs were not being done, rather than you wanting upgrades to equipment which could not be offered as quickly as you required.

15.   I see that you made a complaint to Gary Barlow and others on 4 August 2020, and others, saying that you were complaining because your house had not been repaired after well over 18 months for some jobs and more than six months for others. You set out detailed complaints and observations.

15.1.   Your Housing Assistant had not been in touch since January to reply to your original letter of complaint. You said "*I will have the money for the arrears when it comes to the court date but I refuse to pay the rent for this dump of a place in Anytown Borough Council insisted on taking me to court for and I will call for the rent arrears to be set off against the damages disrepairs. I want this letter to be forwarded to the Ombudsman or to be explained to the proper complaints procedure to take Anytown Borough Council to court. I have pictures of the state they left my bathroom from well over a year ago when the job was first raised by the same surveyor who came this year, then I have witnesses who would either work or are contracted by Anytown Borough Council who are prepared to testify will write a statement about the way my house has been neglected. One very unhappy and disgusted council tenant.*"

15.2.   I imagine that you had received some legal advice from the Law Centre, who would probably have said that you should ask to reduce your arrears by saying you had disrepair at the flat.

15.3.   On 18 August 2020 Edward Jones replied to your complaint, saying that there had been some access difficulties and telling you that he had asked the contractor to arrange some dates to carry out various works to the flat.

15.3.1.   He said "*I was surprised to read that you are still experiencing problems with getting repairs done in your home, and that for some you have been waiting over 18 months. I checked our system and could find no reported repairs to the floor and ceilings going back that far. I also noted that according to our records we do seem to have access problems to your home over two years we have had the following incidents: (Mr Jones then set out nine appointments which had been missed by the tenant.) I can only apologise for the non-attendance by us on 25 July 2020, you should have received a telephone call or text message informing you that the appointment had been cancelled but quite clearly this was not the case."*

15.3.2. He told you that he had arranged with the contractor to replace two spindles, adjust and ease the front door, cut out and repair the flooring in the lounge, ease and adjust the lounge window and check for water ingress, fit new flooring in the kitchen and ease windows in the bedrooms and bathroom, scraped back the Artex and replace it in the kitchen and lounge and remove old tiles at the base of the stairs, screed the floor and lay nonslip flooring and make good around the window at the top of the stairs.

15.3.3. The contractor had been unable to contact you.

16. On 14 December 2020 Lisa Curtis emailed you saying *"please be advised as per your recent communications with our housing inspector, that our tradesmen will be attending your property this morning to action the necessary plastering works to the hallway and lounge."* You replied saying *"I think the one who needs to be advised is you as your level of understanding is very low. You are supposed to liaise with me as to when the appointments are made. You have not contacted me once and made the appointments on your own without me agreeing to 1 of them. I think your communication system is a failure because I have informed the surveyor three times now that I am not available until after 11 AM and if you would contacted me as instructed by the surveyor last week you would have saved the taxpayer money and sending workers at 9 AM...."*

17. On 6 January 2021 you emailed again in response to an email from Brent Rogers of 5 January, which said that carpenters had visited but had been told "by a male hanging out of the window that today had been cancelled by yourself", saying that contractors had attended on 5 January but you had not agreed to that appointment and was unable to allow them access. You were clearly fed up with appointments being mixed up. You were also fed up with another heating engineer coming around and discussing heating. Lots of

engineers and surveyors had apparently done nothing. You also complained that the kitchen floor had not been renewed and the "*excuse of a new kitchen is rubbish as the floors put for repairs in May*". You said that you were "*utterly fed up with you guys... Making appointments for things that are irrelevant, like splinters in the stairs, a vent cover in the corridor and someone again to look at the heaters... What about putting central heating and fixing the window so I don't have to spend a fortune in heating the draughty flat!*"

18. I get the impression that the repairs department would not accept that the problems have been caused by them, but by you being difficult of access. I don't believe it's necessary to make a formal finding one way or the other in that regard, because I'm concentrating more on the overall picture in relation to each item of work. Attached to this letter as "Addendum to stage 3 complaint" is a document showing details of the missed appointments.

19. Throughout the period above there was lots of discussion about your rent arrears, which were and are rising at an alarming rate. They were already £2,144.21 in August 2020 and no further payment was made until 1 November 2020 when you paid £400. At the hearing of 10 October 2020, the District Judge directed that "*during the adjournment the defendant shall pay current rent as it falls due*". You did not appeal that order. You have remained in breach of the order but paid occasional amounts towards the arrears.

20. By 26 June 2021 arrears were £3,066 and on 22 March they were £3,247.14. Regrettably the position is worsened by the fact that the DWP say that the Council has been overpaid Universal Credit of £1,102.97. I think you have accepted that you cannot challenge that. The Council will have to repay this money to the DWP. Rent arrears are **I have attached as Addendum 2 details of the rent and Universal Credit situation since 2 October 2021.**

My conclusions

21. Looking at the many documents on your file, I believe that you have some good reason to feel that the service offered by the Council has not been as good as it could have been. However I do not feel that it

is entirely at fault, as the number of appointments you miss is higher than the norm. I also believe that some of the issues you have complained about could not be classed as "repairs" and so it was sometimes difficult for anything to be done about them. Money needed to be made available from capital improvements budgets and the like, rather than just getting repairs ordered. Looking at it in the round, there is no doubt that communication could have been better at times, but whenever there is a situation with lots of complaints about the property, some of which are things that can be addressed and some not, it's difficult to satisfy a tenant completely.

22. Bringing together the separate amounts I've listed above, I'm prepared to offer you compensation in the form of a reduction of your now significant rent arrears, totalling **£1,500**. This would, if you accept it, bring the amount of arrears down to **£1,747.14 as at today's date.**

23. This amount is offered as a full and final settlement of the complaint you have raised. It would mean that you would not need to carry on with the legal Counterclaim you made against the Council unless you believe that the offer does not compensate you enough. There is nothing to stop you from continuing with the Counterclaim though. As I said above, it is most unfortunate that when Mr Brannan wrote to you in August 2016 telling you that you could complain further to me, you did not do so. The subsequent legal proceedings would probably have been avoided if you had made a further, formal complaint.

24. If you agree with my decision, please fill in and sign the attached Form of Acceptance and I will arrange for the credit to be made to your rent account. In the future I would hope that you can buy dialogue and negotiation with your Housing Officer and the Repairs Department sort out repairs issues as they arise and, if you're not happy, complain immediately rather than some time later.

Yours Sincerely

Jessica Burdle, Chief Executive, Anytown Borough Council

APPENDIX TWO

EXAMPLE DEFENCE

This is single-spaced to compress it, but pleadings must be in 12 point font with 1.5 spacing. I have put in every possible point I could think of, so it is much longer than most Defences would be in practice.

IN THE COUNTY COURT SITTING AT
ANYTOWN CIVIL JUSTICE CENTRE

CLAIM NUMBER

MRS TENANT

MR TENANT

CLAIMANTS

AND

ANYTOWN CITY LANDLORD

DEFENDANT

DEFENCE

---

1. Paragraph 1 is admitted. The Claimants have been tenants of the Property since 5 June 2015 pursuant to a tenancy agreement signed by them on 1 June 2015. They have occupied it with their son, who is now aged 28.

2. Paragraph 2 is admitted. Further:

2.1. such obligations are subject to the condition that repairs should be done within a reasonable time of notification, and to a reasonable standard having regard to the age, character and prospective life of the dwelling house and the locality in which it is situated.

2.2. by Clause 10 of the tenancy agreement, it was an express term of the said tenancy that the Tenants would immediately report to the Landlord any blocked drains, defects in the structure and all other repairs required on the part of the Landlord and that the Tenants would refer to the leaflet "Getting Repairs Done" and follow the procedure set out therein in the event of the occurrence of disrepair.

2.3. the Tenants were under a duty to use the premises in a tenant-like manner.

2.4. By clause 13 of the tenancy agreement the Tenants were and remain under a duty to allow the Landlord access at all reasonable times to carry out inspections and any works considered necessary.

2.5. In determining the standard of repair required by the covenant implied by the Landlord and Tenant Act 1985 ("the 1985 Act") and under section 4 of the Defective Premises Act 1972 ("the 1972 Act"), the Court is entitled to have regard to the age, character and prospective life of the dwelling house and the locality in which it is situated, pursuant to Section 11 (3) of the Landlord and Tenant Act 1985.

2.6. As to section 9 and 10 of the 1985 Act, it is admitted that the Defendant is obliged to maintain the Property so that it is fit for human habitation, subject to the matters set out in section 9A (2) and (3).

2.7. It is admitted that section 4 the 1972 Act imposed a duty on the Landlord to take such care as was reasonable in all the circumstances to see that the Tenants were reasonably safe from damage to their property caused by a relevant defect and averred that such relevant defect means a defect in the state of the premises arising from or continuing because of an act or omission by the Defendant which constituted a failure by it to carry out its obligation to the Tenants for the maintenance or repair of the premises. It is denied that the Landlord was under any further duty to the Tenants. Further the standard of repair required is limited to that required by section 11 of the Landlord and Tenant Act 1985.

2.8. It is denied that the pleading in respect of section 4 of the 1972 Act is relevant so far as it relates to taking care to ensure that personal injury is not caused to the Tenants by a relevant defect, there being no subsequent allegation that the Tenants have suffered any personal injury as a result of such defects.

3. As to paragraph 3, it is admitted that the Defendant has not supplied a copy of the tenancy agreement to the Claimants. The Tenants should have in their possession a copy of the tenancy agreement as handed to them upon commencement of the tenancy.

3.1. Further, the Tenants have always been and are entitled to request a copy of that document outside the legal process and at no cost to themselves.

3.2. It is denied that the Tenants are entitled to seek disclosure through the Pre-Action Protocol for Housing Conditions claims until they have complied with paragraph 4.1 of the Protocol and have attempted alternative dispute resolution, or provided good reason as to why they should not at least attempt a cost free and speedy resolution to their concerns.

3.3. Pursuant to paragraph 4.2 of the Pre-Action Protocol, alternatives for social housing tenants include the repairs, complaints and/or arbitration procedure as the first step and, if that does not resolve matters, recourse to the Housing Ombudsman.

3.4. By a letter dated 30 January 2020 the Landlord informed the Claimants' Solicitors that they were obliged to consider alternative dispute resolution and referred them to the Landlord's formal complaints procedure, warning them of adverse consequences for failure to do so provided inter alia by paragraphs 13-16 of the Practice Direction Relating to Pre-Action Conduct and Protocols.

3.5. The Defendant then put into operation Stage 1 of its

227

formal Complaints Process. It investigated the history of reports of defects and works done and concluded that certain works should be carried out, in accordance with the plans already made by its repairs team. It did not recommend the payment of any compensation because no breach of duty or service failure had been found in the investigation.

3.6. By a further letter dated 23 February 2020, the Landlord informed the Tenants that if they were unhappy with the finding by the Landlord within Stage 1 of the complaints procedure, they should take their complaint further, using Stage 2 of the procedure.

3.7. The Claimants' Solicitors ignored the request to consider and attempt alternative dispute resolution and, in a further letter dated 1 March 2020, disclosed a report by a Mr Anthony Smith, a Surveyor who had, according to the Claimants' Solicitors been instructed as a *"Single Joint Expert"*, despite no such instruction having been given by the Defendant. Further, it has been prepared without any reference to:

3.7.1. the records of the concerns of which the Defendant has been notified by the Claimants, which reflect:

3.7.1.1. the timing and extent of such notification and

3.7.1.2. the nature of their concerns as they were contemporaneously expressed by the Claimants themselves;

3.7.2. the repairs and improvements history as carried out by the Landlord;

3.7.3. the extent of any effect on the amenity of the Claimants of any alleged defect;

3.7.4. the effect of the occupation by the Claimants themselves on the state of repair and condition of the Property, for instance the manner in which the Tenants have used the Property, the condition and state of cleanliness in which they have kept it, the degree to which they have carried out or failed to carry out any minor repairs or improvements themselves and the standard to which they have decorated it;

3.7.5. section 11 (3) of the 1985 Act, so that no account has been taken of the age, character and locality of the dwelling house, or of its prospective life,

and it is therefore denied that the opinions expressed in the report should be given any weight by the court, save to record the physical condition in which Mr Smith found the Property during his visit on a date unknown prior to 1 March 2020.

3.8. By letter dated 7 March 2020, the Landlord reminded the Claimants' Solicitors of their obligation to advise their clients to consider alternative dispute resolution and queried the circumstances of their instruction.

3.9. Further, since the Defendant received the Letter of Claim, the Claimants have persistently refused to give access to its employees to inspect and to remedy any defects which might be found, telling the Defendant that their solicitors had advised them to refuse such access.

3.10.On 8 May 2020, the Claimants' Solicitors issued a premature, unnecessary and vexatious claim, despite the clear requests to consider ADR referred to above, and their knowledge that the Landlord was attempting to enter to inspect and carry out. In the circumstances the claim amounts to a serious breach of the Pre-Action Protocol and the Practice Direction and is an abuse of process.

3.11.The Claimants have served notice of funding by way of conditional fee agreement, which is not backed by any insurance policy, so that they remain personally liable for the costs incurred by their Solicitors.

3.12.The remainder of this Defence is pleaded without prejudice to the Landlord's contention that these proceedings should be struck as they are an abuse of process and, or otherwise likely to obstruct the just disposal of the proceedings and because there has been a failure to comply with the said Practice Direction and Pre-Action Protocol.

4. Paragraph 4 is admitted, save that it is denied that the obligation requires or imposes any further duty than that under the 1985 Act or within the tenancy. The implied covenant not to derogate from grant is not relevant to this claim.

5. Save as admitted herein below, paragraph 5 is denied.

PARTICULARS OF DEFECTS ADMITTED AND OF DENIALS

5.1. Throughout the duration of the tenancy the Claimants have reported defects and problems experienced in the Property, as set out in the repairs records, full particulars of which exceed three folios and will be served if this claim proceeds.

5.2. The Defendant has an extensive Estates department, which maintains approximately 15,000 properties in and around Anytown. It is specifically denied that repairs are not carried out because of impecuniosity, as pleaded by the Claimants. In administering its housing stock, a landlord is entitled to have regard to the likely cost/benefit ratio of any works of repair or improvement in its determination of the appropriate standard of repair.

5.3. On 4 March 2019 the Claimants complained to the Defendant that they were unhappy with the condition of their kitchen and of their bathroom and sought replacement of both. The Defendant responded by email dated 14 March 2019 and informed them that a full survey of the Property was to be ordered. Through administrative error the survey was not carried out until 12 June 2019.

5.4. By email dated 18 June 2019 the Defendant informed the Claimants that the survey had revealed the need to carry out damp proofing works and re-plastering works behind the kitchen units and to fill any gaps in the plaster behind the units.

5.5. In the same email the Defendant informed the Claimant that it was to carry out the following works:

5.5.1. on 26 September 2019, rewiring of the kitchen remain and works to the distribution board;

5.5.2. on 28 September 2019, refitting of the kitchen after those works; the units were not to be replaced but repaired with new plinths, replacement drawers and easing of all doors, and with better support to the worktops;

5.5.3. damp contractors were engaged to replace the extractor fan in the kitchen and in the bathroom with an upgraded version of those fans (such fans not being in disrepair but being replaced by upgraded and more modern versions, such that they were works of improvement rather than repair within the meaning of the 1985 Act);

5.5.4. the bath was to be replaced after the kitchen work was completed and a mould wash to the bathroom ceiling was to be considered after the bath had been replaced (it being admitted that the bath was in need of replacement, but not that it caused any significant loss of amenity, and otherwise it being denied that such works were works which remedied any defect within the meaning of the 1985 Act;

5.5.5. loft insulation was to be investigated and improved (such works not being within the ambit of the 1985 Act, in that they were improvements to the design of the Property).

5.6. By reply email dated 18 October 2019 the Claimants repeated their request for the replacement of the kitchen units because of the dampness. They made a further complaint, which was further investigated in October 2019.

5.7. Following such investigation, the Landlord decided that the kitchen would not be replaced as it was still fit for purpose and there was no structural damp in the wall behind the units, nor was there any mould or water damage to the backs of the units. In January 2020 contractors employed by the Landlord, "ACME Damp Control", repaired some damp areas in the kitchen wall behind. That damp was caused by condensation generated by two unvented tumble dryers belonging to the Claimants, situated in front of the damaged wall. Such damage amounts to an 'act of waste', for which the Claimants have not yet been recharged.

5.8. A decision was made to replace the sink base unit and repair the existing, together with a section of worktop to the left-hand side of the sink where there was some water damage where the mastic seal had broken down.

5.9. The Claimant were informed that their kitchen would be replaced in 2022, pursuant to the "Keystone" planned works kitchen program, which the First Claimant accepted orally at the time.

5.10. Accordingly, it is denied that the damp in the kitchen was caused by a defect within the meaning of section 11 of the 1985 Act, the Defendant's case being that the cause of such damp (and that of a small area in the lounge) has not yet been definitively ascertained.

5.11. Further, when contractors attended the Property in October 2019, they discovered that they needed to rewire it completely because they found further faults on several circuits which they could not rectify. The rewiring was due to begin on 16 January 2020 but on 9 January 2020 the Claimants informed the Defendant that they would refuse access for the rewiring because they had obtained an independent damp survey which alleged that the whole house was damp and they had instructed solicitors.

5.12. Since that date, the Claimants have allowed the Defendant into the Property on two occasions but have refused further access, either for inspections or for the carrying out of works.

5.13. As a result of the refusal of access and consequential breach of tenancy on the part of the Claimants, the Defendant was and remains unable to carry out such works as are necessary, or even to inspect the Property to determine what is necessary.

5.14. Further details of defects found and admitted are contained either in the report of Mr Paul Surveyor, dated March 2017 and attached as Appendix 1.

5.15. Once the works specified by Mr Surveyor and those before him have been carried out, the Landlord will be able to make a judgement whether any further works are necessary to alleviate any disrepair at the Property. Such a decision is a matter for the Landlord, rather than for the Claimants or their Solicitors or Surveyor, save that the Landlord as landlord may take into account the views and opinions of others in deciding how best to remedy any disrepair found at the Property.

5.16. In repairing such defects, the landlord of a property is entitled to approach works according to good Estate management principles in a reasonable manner, carrying out such works as it considers necessary and proportionate and, for instance, not being obliged to replace in the first instance rather than repair when necessary and to replace only when repairs prove ineffective.

5.17. Accordingly, it is admitted that, between March and October 2016 the Defendant was aware of alleged defects with the kitchen and the bathroom of the Property as set out in the Claimants' complaint concerning the condition of those rooms but not otherwise. It is further admitted that upon inspection in October it was found necessary to carry out works to both those rooms, but not admitted that such works reflect the existence of "disrepair" within the meaning of the 1985 Act.

5.18. If, which is not admitted for the purposes of these proceedings, any liability in damages for loss of amenity arises as a result of the Defendant's failure to proceed with the inspection in March 2016, such failure can be investigated within Stage 2 of the complaints process and, if fault is found in the service level offered by the Defendant, if compensation can be offered to the Claimants within that cost-free process.

5.19. Further, if during the Stage 2 complaints process further allegations are made by the Claimants of any breach of duty or failure in service levels on the part of the Defendant, such complaints can be considered and adjudicated upon within that process, at no cost to either party and without involving lawyers. If the Claimants remained dissatisfied with the result of their complaint within Stage

2, they can proceed to Stage 3 and/or to complain to the Ombudsman.

5.20.If, which is denied, the Claimants are entitled to any damages for loss of amenity, it is averred that recovery by way of this claim is unnecessary and premature and that such claims should not be permitted to proceed until alternative dispute resolution has been attempted.

5.21.Further, the Defendant will rely on section 11(3) of the Landlord and Tenant Act 1985 in that the standard of repair was reasonable having regard to the age, character and prospective life of the dwelling house and the locality it which it is situated and taking into account particularly that the Claimants occupy the Property pursuant to a secure tenancy at a rent which is substantially less than the open market rent of privately owned housing in the area.

6.   As to paragraph 6, it is admitted that the Claimants have reported defects as set out in the records of such reports contained in the computerised repairs files, full particulars of which exceed three folios and will be disclosed if this claim proceeds to a trial.

PARTICULARS OF DENIAL

6.1. As pleaded above, it is admitted that Mr Atkinson inspected the Property and found it in the physical condition set out in his report.

6.2. To the extent that there are differences between the opinion of Mr Paul Jones, Surveyor for the Defendant and Mr Atkinson, the Defendant relies on the evidence and opinion of Mr Surveyor, as it is entitled to do as landlord.

6.3. The instruction of Mr Atkinson was unnecessary and premature, the Claimants having failed to pursue the complaints procedure properly or at all.

6.4. If, following further investigation, the Claimants are found to have suffered unnecessary loss of amenity as a result of any breach of duty on the part of the Defendant, they should be compensated within the complaints procedure.

6.5. It is admitted that, if they remain dissatisfied with any offers made pursuant to Stage 2 or Stage 3 of the complaints process, or by the Ombudsman, the Claimants are entitled to proceed with litigation and to rely upon the findings of Mr Atkinson.

6.6. The Defendant reserves its position in relation to the findings by Mr Atkinson so far as they differ from those of Mr Surveyor and will plead further only if necessary in the event that this matter is not struck out, and after any stay imposed by the Court has expired.

6.7. It is not admitted that the Claimants have suffered discomfort and inconvenience because the house has been damp and has smelt of damp for an inordinately long period of time as a result of any breach of duty on the part of the Defendant.

6.8. The activities of the Claimants have caused/created significant condensation dampness, as set out in the report by Paul Jones. Further, some condensation dampness has been caused/created by defects in design rather than defects in the structure of the Property, and are not actionable under the 1985 Act.

6.9. If, which is not admitted, any dampness was caused by any breach of duty on the part of the Defendant, the effect of such dampness is insignificant compared to the effect of dampness caused by such condensation and any damage suffered by the Claimants has been and is "de minimis" for the purposes of any claim in damages.

6.10. It is specifically denied that the Defendant has refused, persistently or at all, to carry out repair work to merely as alleged, or that it has treated the Claimants in a contemptuous manner or in any way other than as secure tenants entitled to seek the repair of their Property pursuant to statute and under the tenancy agreement. It is denied that the Claimants are entitled to any higher standard of repair or remedy than that provided by the Act or the tenancy agreement, so that it is denied for example that they are entitled to insist on the installation of a new kitchen or bathroom, as claimed by them.

6.11.Further, to the extent that the works carried out and/or ordered by the Defendant involve works of improvement, there is no obligation on the Defendant to carry out such works and no liability in damages arises from any failure to order or to carry them out.

6.12.The Defendant has investigated, identified and remedied, or attempted to remedy the causes of dampness and mould growth so far as they are caused by disrepair and has gone beyond its contractual and statutory duties in the remedy of design defects, as set out in the records of repairs and above.

6.13.As to the claim for special damages, it is denied that the Claimants have suffered any damage as a result of any breach of duty on the part of the Defendant. By reason of the matters set out above, it is denied that the Defendant has been in breach of its duty under the tenancy or otherwise.

6.14.If, which is denied, the Defendant has failed to repair the property in accordance with its duty it is denied that any such failure has caused any damage which is more than "de minimis", as pleaded above. Further, the Claimants have failed wholly to mitigate any damage being suffered by refusing the Defendant access to carry out inspections and repairs.

6.15.If, which is not admitted, the Claimants have suffered any loss of amenity, damage to property or other damage, such damage was caused by the Claimants' own 'acts of waste' or other failures to heat/ventilate/use the Property properly so as to avoid the formation of condensation damp and resulting mould, and they have failed to mitigate their loss.

PARTICULARS OF ACTS OF WASTE/FAILURE TO MITIGATE

In particular the Claimants:

6.16.have failed to give notice of the existence of defects within the Defendant's repairing obligations properly or at all;

6.17. if, which is denied, the Claimants did give notice of such defects, they have failed to follow-up when works have not been carried out to their satisfaction;

6.18. have used an unvented condensing tumble dryer in the Property and have dried clothes on the radiators, significantly increasing the moisture levels in the Property;

6.19. have spilt water in the bathroom in excessive quantities;

6.20. failed to ensure that the bathroom window was open during or after bathing activities

6.21. have failed to clean off condensation and/or mould as it has formed on surfaces in the property;

6.22. have failed otherwise to use the extractor fans fitted in the property properly and have removed the fuses from them;

6.23. have failed otherwise to ventilate the property by opening windows as necessary;

6.24. have failed otherwise to comply with their obligation to use the property in a tenant-like manner;

6.25. if, which is denied, after notification by the Claimants, such repairs as were necessary were not done within a reasonable period of time, they have failed to give further notice to the Defendant properly or at all and to follow the repairs reporting and the formal complaints procedure, which will be referred to at trial.

6.26. If the Claimants had pursued the formal complaints procedure through Stage 2 or Stage 3, even if there were "disrepair" in the Property within the meaning of the Act or tenancy, and the Defendant had failed to repair it, such disrepair would have been detected and remedied by that process and the Claimants would not have continued to suffer any loss.

6.27. The Claimants' claim to any special damages is denied and they are put to proof thereof by the production of receipts or the exact date and place of purchase of all items set out therein and the facts on which they rely to prove that the items were damaged by any breach of duty rather than condensation dampness.

6.28. The Claimants are not entitled to specific performance of the repairing covenants, as since January 2017 they have refused to allow the Defendant access to inspect and repair save on the occasions set out in the evidence to be provided.

7. Paragraph 7 is denied for the reasons set out above. The Claimants' surveyor did not find that the Property was unfit human habitation and section 9A the 1985 Act is irrelevant, as is section 4 of the DPA 1972, there being no allegations of damage to property or injury to persons.

8. As to paragraph 8, the contents of paragraph 3 to 6 above are repeated and it is averred that litigation is entirely unnecessary and that the Claimants have themselves caused any continuing loss of amenity by refusing access to the Defendant to carry out inspections and repairs. These proceedings should be dismissed, or in the alternative, stayed pending the outcome of that alternative dispute resolution.

9. As to paragraph 9, the Claimants' belief is not relevant. The factual history as set out above reflects the nature of the breach on the part of the Claimants' Solicitors failure to comply with the requirements of the Pre-Action Protocol and Practice Direction to undertake alternative dispute resolution if practicable.

10. As to paragraph 10, the issue of these proceedings was entirely unnecessary for the reasons given above and the Defendant has on numerous occasions made proposals that the Claimants should pursue Stage 2 of the complaints process. The Defendant repeats that request, relying on the law set out in the Claimants' own Particulars of Claim.

11. As to the Prayer:

11.1. it is denied that the Claimants are entitled to proceed with unnecessary litigation in circumstances where an alternative and cost-free remedy is available to the Claimants.

11.2. In the circumstances, it is denied that the Claimants are entitled to any damages at this point in time. If that alternative dispute resolution is unsuccessful and the Claimants remain dissatisfied with the remedies offered by the Defendant, it is admitted that the Claimants may be entitled to modest compensation for the delay in arranging a survey between March and October 2016 (and/or for any further breaches of duty or failures of service detected during the complaints process), but averred that such compensation would and should have been sought within the cost-free complaints process, so that no costs would be payable if this claim proceeds without completion of that process;

11.3. it is denied that the Claimants are entitled to an order for specific performance, as the failure to carry out works at the Property arises as a result of the Claimants' own refusal of access, rather than any refusal by the Defendant to carry out works of repair and/or improvement as necessary and as already ordered by the Defendant in 2016;

11.4. The Claimants' entitlement to interest is denied, no sums being due in damages;

11.5. the claim should be allocated to the Small Claims Track, there being no arguable claim for injunctive relief or for damages in excess of £1,000.

12. Further and in any event, the Claimants' claim is statute barred in so far as any act or default occurred more than six years prior to the issue of the claim, or, to the extent that any allegation of physical injury is made, three years prior to the date of issue.

13. Save as herein admitted the Claimants' claim is denied as if set out and specifically traversed seriatim.

DEFENDANT NAME

STATEMENT OF TRUTH

The Defendant believe that the facts stated in this Defence are true. I understand that proceedings for contempt of court may be brought against anyone who makes, or causes to be made, a false statement in a document verified by a statement of truth without an honest belief in its truth.

I am duly authorised by the Defendant to sign this statement

Full name: ....

Name of Defendant's Solicitor's firm:
Anytown City Landlord Legal Services

Signed ....   position or office held: Solicitor

Dated this .... Day of ....20..

By

....

To the Claimants

And to the District Judge

BIBLIOGRAPGHY

Dowding & Reynolds (sixth edition 2017), N Dowding and K Reynolds Sweet & Maxwell/Thomson Reuters

Housing Conditions, Tenants' Rights (Sixth Edition, 2019) HHJ J Luba, C O'Donnell and G Peaker, Legal Action Group

INDEX

MORE BOOKS BY
LAW BRIEF PUBLISHING

A selection of our other titles available now:-

'A Practical Guide to Solicitor and Client Costs – 2nd Edition' by Robin Dunne
'Constructive Dismissal – Practice Pointers and Principles' by Benjimin Burgher
'A Practical Guide to Religion and Belief Discrimination Claims in the Workplace' by Kashif Ali
'A Practical Guide to the Law of Medical Treatment Decisions' by Ben Troke
'Fundamental Dishonesty and QOCS in Personal Injury Proceedings: Law and Practice' by Jake Rowley
'A Practical Guide to the Law in Relation to School Exclusions' by Charlotte Hadfield & Alice de Coverley
'A Practical Guide to Divorce for the Silver Separators' by Karin Walker
'The Right to be Forgotten – The Law and Practical Issues' by Melissa Stock
'A Practical Guide to Planning Law and Rights of Way in National Parks, the Broads and AONBs' by James Maurici QC, James Neill et al
'A Practical Guide to Election Law' by Tom Tabori
'A Practical Guide to the Law in Relation to Surrogacy' by Andrew Powell
'A Practical Guide to Claims Arising from Fatal Accidents – 2nd Edition' by James Patience
'A Practical Guide to the Ownership of Employee Inventions – From Entitlement to Compensation' by James Tumbridge & Ashley Roughton
'A Practical Guide to Asbestos Claims' by Jonathan Owen & Gareth McAloon
'A Practical Guide to Stamp Duty Land Tax in England and Northern Ireland' by Suzanne O'Hara
'A Practical Guide to the Law of Farming Partnerships' by Philip Whitcomb

These books and more are available to order online direct from the publisher at www.lawbriefpublishing.com, where you can also read free sample chapters. For any queries, contact us on 0844 587 2383 or mail@lawbriefpublishing.com.

Our books are also usually in stock at www.amazon.co.uk with free next day delivery for Prime members, and at good legal bookshops such as Wildy & Sons.

We are regularly launching new books in our series of practical day-to-day practitioners' guides. Visit our website and join our free newsletter to be kept informed and to receive special offers, free chapters, etc.

You can also follow us on Twitter at www.twitter.com/lawbriefpub.

Printed in Great Britain
by Amazon

46545510R00156